Laying
the
Ladder
Down

ଏ

A volume in

the series

Critical

Perspectives

on Modern

Culture

edited by David Gross &

William M. Johnston

The Emergence of

Cultural Holism

Betty Jean Craige

The University of Massachusetts Press

Amherst

Laying the Ladder Down

Copyright © 1992

by The University of

Massachusetts Press

All rights reserved

Printed in the United States

of America

LC 92—10934

ISBN 0-87023-805-1 (cloth);

806-x (pbk.)

Designed by Richard Hendel

Set in Minion by

Keystone Typesetting, Inc.

Printed and bound by

Thomson-Shore, Inc.

Library of Congress Cataloging-in-Publication Data

Craige, Betty Jean.

Laying the ladder down : the emergence of cultural holism /

Betty Jean Craige.

p.   cm. — (Critical perspectives of modern culture)

Includes bibliographical references and index.

ISBN 0—87023—805—1 (alk. paper). — ISBN 0—87023—806—x

(pbk. : alk. paper)

1. Culture.   2. Holism.   3. Pluralism (Social sciences)

4. Ethnicity.   5. Equality.   I. Title.   II. Series.

HM101.C74   1992

306—dc20   92—10934

                                                        CIP

British Library Cataloguing in Publication data are

available.

TO GENE ODUM

Contents

Acknowledgments

I have dedicated *Laying the Ladder Down* to Gene Odum, who over the years has shown me how to think about things "ecologically"; not only did he inspire me to write this book, but he read every chapter critically and offered valuable suggestions. I thank him and his wife, Martha, both wonderful friends, for their interest in my work.

I thank my very generous colleague Charles Doyle, who read the manuscript in its entirety (parts of it several times), for his meticulous attention to the details, for the almost daily conversations about the political issues I wanted to address, and for the book's title. It was Charlie who thought that *Laying the Ladder Down* might catch the eye of more readers than *The Shift from a Dualistic, Atomistic, and Hierarchical Model of Reality to a Holistic Model.* I am most grateful for his insight.

Frederick Ferré and Frank Golley also graciously read the manuscript and provided excellent advice; I am indebted to Frank for teaching me about "deep ecology" and to Frederick for introducing me to the current debates over environmental ethics. Early on, when I was just beginning to outline the book, Wyatt Anderson helped me to see how Darwin's abandonment of the typological species concept was central to the argument I was trying to make; I appreciate the encouragement both Wyatt and his wife, Margaret, gave me during the long process of writing.

Other friends from various disciplines at the University of Georgia have been indispensable as well. So I thank Ron Bogue, Vinay Dharwadker, Ed Halper, Gene Helfman, Ed Larson, Judy Meyer, Kent Middleton, Bernie Patten, and Anne Williams for orienting me to the current issues in their fields of expertise and for reading sections of the manuscript.

I thank William M. Johnston and Paul Lauter for helping me to clarify my argument, Baird Callicott for reviewing the chapter on environmentalism, in which his ideas figure prominently, and Charlie Jansen for reviewing the chapter on the "backlash." I thank Valerie Greenberg for giving me the book on animal rights that several years ago awakened me to the range of "liberation" movements in our time.

I thank my graduate students, in particular JoAnne Juett and Laura Thomson, for alerting me to articles and books they thought might be relevant to "laying the ladder down."

I thank the Modern Language Association for permission to reprint material from a guest column I published in the May 1991 issue of *PMLA*. Finally, I want to express my gratitude to the University of Georgia Research Foundation for supporting the project by giving me the time to write.

❧ Laying
the
Ladder
Down

Introduction

Charles Darwin's opponents in the late nineteenth century reacted to his theory of evolution by natural selection with as much anger as neoconservatives today are reacting to multiculturalism, and for much the same reason. They feared a nonanthropocentric conception of nature in which change is continuous and undirected, because it contradicted their conception of human society as a God-created, and therefore stable, hierarchy. Neoconservatives fear the cultural flux that in recent years has been accelerated in the United States by immigration, integration, and equal opportunity legislation, because it is transforming the nation's traditional identity. In both cases, the vertical social order is threatened.

We are witnessing in many of the controversies of the late twentieth century a conflict between two models of reality: the hierarchical model that has governed Western mentality[1] since the time of the ancient Greeks and a newer, holistic model, anticipated by Darwin and expressed in multiculturalism, environmentalism, and the international peace movement, as well as in relativity, indeterminacy, and general systems theory. One model is static, the other dynamic. Politically, those whose thinking is structured by the former will view social change as disorder, and they will resist it; those whose thinking is structured by the latter will view change as natural, inevitable, and even desirable.

The West's traditional conceptualization of reality we can trace to the fifth century B.C., when Leucippus and Democritus propounded the notion that nature is constituted by discrete particles, or atoms. In the fourth century Plato conceived of reality as divisible into two realms, that of Ideas and that of their appearances in nature. Plato's pupil Aristotle saw nature as a static "scale of ascent." From Aristotle, who ranked the organisms of the natural world according to their degree of "soul," placing animals above plants, mammals above insects, and humans at the top, we inherited a propensity to rank everything, including the races and the sexes. From Plato we inherited both a belief in an unchanging order governing the earth's biological diversity and a propensity to dichotomize everything—into oppositions of spirit and matter, stasis and flux, mind and body, self and world, culture and nature, the intellectual and the political. From Leucippus and Democritus we inherited a tendency to under-

3

stand relationships in terms of mechanical interactions of autonomous entities.[2]

The conceptual rank order supported a vertical social order by making inequality of wealth and privilege seem "natural." On a ladder some would naturally be at the top and others at the bottom. The spirit/matter dualism established oppositional relationships that relegated women, nonwhite races, non-Western peoples, other species, and the land itself to the inferior category of the "material" and thereby justified their exploitation. Within the model, men were considered more rational than women, who had to devote themselves to the natural process of reproduction; whites were considered more intelligent than people of color; the West was considered more civilized than the rest of the world; and, because only human beings were supposed to have souls, humans were considered superior to other species of animals, to plants, to "nature" itself. Superiority carried with it the right to dominate, control, possess, exploit, destroy.

During the past hundred years innumerable battles have been fought between those viewing their experience the traditional way—hierarchically, atomistically, dualistically—and those viewing their experience the new way, holistically. The early battles took place on intellectual terrain; among them were the mid-nineteenth-century debate over the origin of species, the late-nineteenth-century challenge of the impressionists to the realist painters, and the arguments over relativity and indeterminacy in physics. The debate continues in literary criticism, philosophy, theology, medicine, economics, politics, and higher education. The rise of feminism, the passage of civil rights legislation, the increased sensitivity to ethnic differences inside our country and throughout the world, the expansion of the international antiwar movement,[3] and the growth of the environmentalist movement—these events signal the radical transformation of Western culture to a more inclusive, less hierarchical, and therefore (ultimately) less oppressive social order.

Holism, from the Greek *holos* ("whole"), has been defined as follows: "the theory that whole entities, as fundamental and determining components of reality, have an existence other than as the mere sum of their parts" (*Random House Dictionary of the English Language*) and "a theory that the universe and especially living nature is correctly seen in terms of interacting wholes (as of living organisms) that are more than the mere sum of elementary particles" (*Webster's New Collegiate Dictionary*). Jan Christiaan Smuts gave the word currency in his 1926 book *Holism and Evolution*, where he advocated the exploration of matter, life, and mind in relation to each other, rather than as isolable realms of existence.[4] Since then, *holistic* has been applied to approaches and attitudes, in the humanities and the social sciences as well as the sciences, that privilege study of a system over analysis of its parts. I am using the adjective in a very broad sense, to describe social movements, in addition to theories and methodologies, that reject the West's traditional model in favor of nonatomistic explanations for events.

Cultural holism is the name I have given to the vision of human society as an evolving, complex, open system of interdependent cultures and individuals, none of which enjoys absolute superiority to any other, all of which develop in relation to each other and to their nonhuman environment.[5] The cultural holists' perspective is like that of ecologists, for whom nature is an ecosystem whose well-being is affected by the interaction of its diverse constituents.[6] For both, interactions determine the function of the system's parts. In the academy, cultural holists are engaged in interdisciplinary research and teaching in the assumption that the understanding of any aspect of a culture requires an understanding of the whole.[7]

Holism is thus a model of reality and a way of understanding. It is also an ideology, an ideology which in its cultural manifestation is incompatible with absolutism of any sort. Whereas absolutism signifies an intolerance of differences, holism signifies an appreciation of differences, of diversity; whereas absolutism generates competition, holism aspires to cooperation; whereas absolutism implies a resistance to change, holism implies a willing acceptance of change, an understanding of reality as continuous flux.

While recognizing the risks of employing any single term to link such different expressions of the new thinking as multiculturalism and environmentalism, I believe that cultural holism emphasizes what they have in common: a rejection of atomism, dualism, and hierarchical ranking. My aim in *Laying the Ladder Down* is to offer a way to understand the intense discussions of our day in relation to each other. Although I may appear to be simplistically opposing holism to the traditional model, thus introducing a new dichotomy into our analysis of events, I am attempting to show how the emergence of a new model elicits vehement defense of the old.

It is with the holistic concept of interdependence—our mutual dependence as humans in a global society, our symbiotic relationship with other animals and with plants, and our reliance upon the health of our planet—that we can see the failure of the old model to address global problems. We can see now that our habitual neglect of species that we ranked lower than humans, as well as of vast numbers of humans on the globe whom we deemed less "civilized" or "advanced" than ourselves, and our pollution of water, land, and air developed out of the model of dominance. We humans are threatened by global warming, by the depletion of the ozone layer, by the extinction of species whose function in our ecosystem we have yet to comprehend, by the accumulation of nuclear and toxic waste, by pollution of the rivers, lakes, and oceans that directly or indirectly supply our food, by unchecked population growth, and by world war. Our cities are afflicted by drug addiction, violent crime, AIDS, and a burgeoning underclass. AIDS, which initially affected only a particular segment of the population and now affects the whole, demonstrates the holistic axiom that the health of a system requires the health of all its components.

In the new global society the traditionally powerful countries with high per capita incomes are threatened by the underclass of the whole world. Half of the planet's inhabitants are hungry (see "Global Village"). As electronic communication reveals to them the difference between our standard of living and theirs, they will discern that our well-being comes at the expense of theirs, and they will be less and less satisfied with their low rung on the global economic ladder. The powerful countries have used force to maintain the unequal distribution of the world's resources, but in diverting disproportionate amounts of wealth to military purposes they have neglected the social, psychological, and economic vitality of their own citizens.

Global politics and the environmental crisis are sending us the same message that Darwin's biology, Einstein's physics, and ecology have delivered: that we must think holistically. We cannot solve our environmental problems without solving our social problems, because human society and nonhuman nature constitute one system. And we cannot solve either our environmental or our social problems without international cooperation, for the system includes all the earth's lands and peoples. No one country can reverse global warming alone. When representatives of all the nations of the world—not just the representatives of the militarily powerful, the industrialized, or the wealthy—gather to address problems, we learn of the viewpoints, interests, values, and conceptual orders of the nations and cultures we have previously ignored, dominated, or excluded from discussion. It is the expansion of the international discussion, made possible by television, that has converted the world into a global community in which we can perceive our interdependence.

Within the United States civil rights legislation is gradually producing a social order in which the contributions of all are recognized as valuable to the efficient functioning of the whole, a social order we may describe as inclusivist.[8] An inclusivist social order would ideally be characterized by a respect for differences, an appreciation of diversity, a preference for cooperation over competition, equality of educational and economic opportunity, and social responsibility. Its governing concern would be the well-being of *all* its citizens.

Social inclusivism is only one aspect of the holistic model. Another aspect is environmentalism. The emergence of the Green Movement, Earth First, Animal Liberation, and the various groups dedicated to saving the whales, the dolphins, the redwoods, and other endangered species indicates a rejection of the model of conquest that had subjected animals and the earth to human exploitation. Now that our ecosystem is in crisis, we are more sensitive than we have been to the way we have treated our planet and its nonhuman inhabitants. When we come to believe that we humans are but one species among many on earth, with no inherent right to dominate, and that we must all live cooperatively together if we are to survive, then we have laid Aristotle's ladder down.

The West's changing conceptual model is the subject of this book. To avoid implying a simple causality and to illustrate the development of the new order, I am analyzing "conversations" taking place in the media: conversations about sexual and racial equality; about the undergraduate curriculum; about Salman Rushdie, fundamentalism, and censorship; about Robert Mapplethorpe and the National Endowment for the Arts (NEA); about multiculturalism and "political correctness"; and about environmental ethics. These conversations reveal the multiple viewpoints—the multiple systems of values, the multiple understandings of the world—that contend with each other whenever new questions arise. I hope that this method will help readers to interpret and to participate in other conversations now taking place in our metamorphosing world.

Ascending the line of gradation, we come at last to the white European; who being most removed from the brute creation, may, on that account, be considered as the most beautiful of the human race. No one will doubt his superiority of intellectual powers; and I believe it will be found that his capacity is naturally superior also to that of every other man. Where shall we find, unless in the European, that nobly arched head, containing such a quantity of brain, and supported by a hollow conical pillar, entering its center? Where the perpendicular face, the prominent nose, and round projecting chin? Where that variety of features, and fulness of expression; those long, flowing, graceful ringlets; that majestic beard, those rosy cheeks and coral lips? Where that erect posture of the body and noble gait? In what other quarter of the globe shall we find the blush that overspreads the soft features of the beautiful women of Europe, that emblem of modesty, of delicate feelings, and of sense? Where that nice expression of the amiable and softer passions in the countenance; and that general elegance of features and complexion? Where, except on the bosom of the European woman, two such plump and snowy white hemispheres, tipt with vermillion?—Charles White, An Account of the Regular Gradation in Man, *1799*

1 &ampersand; The Ladder

Besides a chauvinism that would appear naive to most twentieth-century readers, the British surgeon and obstetrician Charles White expressed in his study of "man" the presuppositions of his time: the concept that nature was governed by ideal *types*, a concept Plato had introduced with his distinction of the realm of unchangeable *eidos* from that of their appearances; and the view of reality as a scale of ascent.[1] For White there was an ideal type of white European woman, just as there was for the other races, and she had on her bosom two "plump and snowy white hemispheres, tipt with vermillion." Those women who did not measure up he considered deviations from type. Because the types were discrete as well as permanent, they could be ranked; on a scale that extended from "brute creation" through the human species to the white European, White ranked his own race highest.

The merging of Plato's dualism with Aristotle's notion of gradation formed the basis for the early ethnologists' ranking of the races. In Aristotle's philosophy, there was no clear split between spirit and nature. Nature was ordered on a vertical scale that extended from rock to man, and the place of any particular being was determined by its degree of "vitality":

> Nature proceeds little by little from things lifeless to animal life in such a way that it is impossible to determine the exact line of demarcation, nor on which side thereof an intermediate form should lie. Thus, next after lifeless things comes the plant, and of plants one will differ from another as to its amount of apparent vitality; and, in a word, the whole genus of plants, whilst it is devoid of life as compared with an animal, is endowed with life as compared with other corporeal entities. Indeed, as we just remarked, there is observed in plants a continuous scale of ascent towards the animal. (Aristotle 1: 922)

Aristotle ranked the animals according to additional powers—such as the appetitive power, the sensory power, the locomotive power, and thought—and placed humans at the top for being able to think abstractly. He went on to speculate that there might be another order of beings, superior to humans, endowed with even greater intellectual capacity.

Using "soul" as the criterion for superiority, Aristotle ranked male over female. In reproduction, he explained, the female provided the material, which the male then fashioned, contributing to it the soul.[2] Critical of Plato's separation of soul from body, Aristotle argued that the soul was really the "form" of the body; it determined the animal's or the plant's function.

In *Politics* Aristotle asserted that, since nature made nothing in vain, all animals existed for the sake of man.[3] He reasoned further that war was just because it was an art of acquisition, like hunting, which "we ought to practise against wild beasts, and against men who, though intended by nature to be governed, will not submit" (Aristotle 2: 1994). The scale of ascent was therefore a model of domination that justified the exploitation by those high on the ladder of those beneath them; it made the exploitation of women, nonwhite races, technologically unsophisticated societies, animals, and the earth itself appear to be "natural."

The ladder model, which may be traced through the New Testament, Neoplatonism, medieval Christianity, and eighteenth-century European philosophy,[4] remained deeply embedded in Western mentality long after it had ceased to be a description of nature. The dualism of spirit and matter (or mind and body) provided a rationale for ranking humans above "nature," human above brute, bishop above priest, king above commoner, man above woman, and white above colored. The church's doctrine that the most lowly peasant could win a place in heaven by humbly accepting his or her lot on earth stabilized the vertical social order: To rebel against one's station was to challenge the laws of God.

It is the presupposition that difference means difference in worth that produces ranking, whether of species, of races, of nations, of sexes, or of texts. And although it disappeared in the biological sciences with the acceptance of Darwinian evolutionary theory, the idea continues to predominate in Western social attitudes. The recent debate over the undergraduate curriculum is a struggle between those who retain the vertical model for understanding phenomena and those who have adopted a holistic model, a model in which diversity appears to benefit the whole. Because the traditional humanistic education is based on the same model as the ranking of the races and the nations, the opposition to it represents an opposition to traditional racial, ethnic, and national relationships.

Early ethnology may give us insight into the dualism that is at the foundation of American attitudes toward race, sex, and cultural achievement.

❧ The Ranking of the Races

In the middle of the nineteenth century, just before the appearance of Darwin's *Origin of Species*, the Philadelphia firm of J. B. Lippincott published two books that brought to the American public the current research into "ethnology." In 1855, Lippincott issued *Types of Mankind* by J. C. Nott, a physician from Mobile, Alabama, and George R. Gliddon, a former U. S. consul in Cairo who had spent some twenty years in the Middle East; its purpose was to show "that the diversity of races must be accepted by Science as a *fact*" (Nott and Gliddon 56). A year later Lippincott published a translation, under the title *The Moral and Intellectual Diversity of Races*, of the first book of a multivolumed French essay on "the inequality of the human races" (1853) by Count Arthur de Gobineau, a novelist and diplomat who had served the French government in Bern, Hanover, Frankfurt, Tehran, Río de Janeiro, and Stockholm. Nott's appendix cited studies by Samuel Morton, late president of the Academy of Natural Sciences at Philadelphia, showing that "the crania of the white are much larger than those of the dark races" (Gobineau, *Intellectual Diversity* 465).[5]

Ethnology, according to Nott's introduction to *Types of Mankind*, sought to discover what characterized the different races, how a race could undergo change, and "what position in the social scale Providence has assigned to each type of man" (Nott and Gliddon 49). In their book Nott and Gliddon defined *types* as primitive or original forms that were independent of climatic or other physical influence (Nott and Gliddon 80) and argued that the *races*, which were distinct and permanent *species*, had separate origins (Nott and Gliddon 79). At the same time, they upheld the notion of *gradation*, which they called a natural law; they viewed the "lower races of mankind" as "connecting links" between the orangutan and the higher races (Nott and Gliddon 457), and mankind as a whole as "a link in Nature's great chain" (Nott and Gliddon 84).

Gobineau, in his treatise, defined three races and amassed evidence for their fundamental differences.[6] Granting the possibility that the present races may have descended from a primitive, unstable type, at a time when the earth was undergoing great inorganic changes, Gobineau attempted to prove that their characteristics were permanent (Gobineau, *Inequality* 139, *Essai* 149). On the basis of the differences he discerned in their intellectual capacity, personal beauty, and physical strength, as well as in their language, he ranked the white race highest and the negroid race lowest, "at the foot of the ladder," with the yellow race between the two (Gobineau, *Inequality* 205, *Essai* 205). He assumed that difference meant inequality.

In Gobineau's differentiation of races according to their bodily aptitudes we can see the functioning of the spirit/matter dualism, manifested in a culture/nature opposition.

> There is no human being so degraded, so brutish, in whom a twofold instinct, if I may be permitted so to call it, is not manifest; the instinct which incites to the gratification of material wants, and that which leads to higher aspirations. The degree of intensity of either of these two is the first and principal measure of the differences among races. In none, not even in the lowest tribes, are the two instincts precisely balanced. Among some, the physical wants or animal propensities preponderate; in others, these are subordinate to the speculative tendencies—the cravings for the abstract, the supernatural. (Gobineau, *Intellectual Diversity* 264)[7]

Inferiority in sensory ability was a sign of superiority in intellectual ability, because in the individual's economy one or the other had to dominate. Intellectual ability, which distinguished humans from animals, who were identified with nature in the culture/nature dichotomy, provided the main criterion for ranking the races. The white race, said Gobineau, was less gifted sensually than either the black or the yellow, and less absorbed by animal gratifications (Gobineau, *Essai* 207); it was therefore, according to his logic, more genuinely human than the black race, which was closer to nature.

Gobineau's declaration that the Aryans, among the whites, were the most gifted in intellect and the most civilized provided the basis for "Gobinism," the theory that nations degenerated as a consequence of mixing with an inferior race.[8]

Nott and Gliddon saw no contradiction between a belief in types and the more evolutionary notion of racial mixture. In fact, they viewed racial mixture as beneficial to those on the low end of the scale, and they attributed human progress to racial wars, to "conquests and colonizations." Nevertheless, they said, "some of the lowest types are hopelessly beyond the reach even of these salutary stimulants to melioration" (Nott and Gliddon 53).

Herein lies the Aristotelian notion that war is an art to be practiced against those whom nature intended to be governed. Aristotle's scale of being, becoming in practice a model for evaluation, thus made imperialism and slavery appear to be warranted by "the laws of God" (Nott and Gliddon 79). It made the "higher races," who used force against the less "civilized" to acquire wealth, the very wealth that furthered their technological and cultural development, appear more deserving of the earth's bounty than the "lower races."[9] And it made the "lower races" appear incapable of benefiting from any wealth, particularly since they were supposedly governed primarily by their physical instincts. The conquerors and colonizers were the ones capable of appreciating truth, beauty, and riches.

Christian missionaries abstracted from the vertical model a moral imperative to carry the light of salvation to the benighted races. Thirty years after the appearance of *Types of Mankind*, the Reverend Josiah Strong published in New York a book called *Our Country*, in which he declared the Anglo-Saxons to be "the great missionary race" because they embodied "a pure *spiritual* Christianity" (unlike the Catholicism of the Continent) (Strong 160).[10] He wrote:

God has two hands. Not only is he preparing in our civilization the die with which to stamp the nations, but . . . he is preparing mankind to receive our impress.

Is there room for reasonable doubt that this race, unless devitalized by alcohol and tobacco, is destined to dispossess many weaker races, assimilate others, and mold the remainder, until, in a very true and important sense, it has Anglo-Saxonized mankind? (Strong 178)

Strong found support for his argument in a passage of *The Descent of Man*, where Darwin attributed "the wonderful progress of the United States, as well as the character of the people," to natural selection.[11] Strong saw no contradiction between Darwin's nontheistic, nonteleological theory of evolution and his own conviction of the white race's divinely appointed purpose. Recognizing that the "unoccupied arable lands of the earth are limited," he announced that the world was about to enter a new stage of its history: "the final competition of races, for which the Anglo-Saxon is being schooled" (Strong 174–175).

> Then this race of unequaled energy, with all the majesty of numbers and the might of wealth behind it . . . having developed peculiarly aggressive traits calculated to impress its institutions upon mankind, will spread itself over the earth. (Strong 175)

Many of those who wrote about race in the latter half of the nineteenth century appropriated Darwin's idea of natural selection to support their thesis of white superiority, but others used the words of the Old Testament. Although the common eighteenth-century belief that the blackness of the African race came from Noah's curse on Ham's descendants had been discredited,[12] some people found other explanations for racial difference that they thought were consistent with Genesis. In the United States, after the Civil War, whites hostile to the enfranchisement of former slaves produced a number of biblical theories about the Negro race's origin, including the pre-Adamite theory that the Negro had entered Noah's ark "as a beast" (Payne 21).[13]

Ashley Montagu has argued that the very idea of race was deliberately created in relation to the African slave trade by "an exploiting class which was seeking to maintain and defend its privileges against what was profitably regarded as an inferior social caste" (Montagu, *Man's Most Dangerous Myth* 39). The combination of the slaves' distinctive color, their illiteracy, and their dependence upon whites, he says, validated for the general public the elaborate theories proposed by the ethnologists. In other words, the effects of social circumstances masqueraded as inherent biological qualities signifying low rank on the scale of ascent.

Although Montagu's story of the way the concept of Negro inferiority benefited the ruling class is persuasive, his assertion that the concept was created for that end is disputable. It is more likely that the Western habit of hierarchical, atomistic thinking predisposed ethnologists, when confronted with the myriad varieties of humankind Europeans had recently discovered in America, Africa, Asia, and the South Seas, to define the races typologically and to rank them. The ethnologists shared the Aristotelian presupposition that difference means difference in worth. For all of them, apparent differences in head size or shape, skin color, hair, or custom indicated relative positions on a vertical scale of values and consequently a fundamental human "inequality." Their explanations for racial differences reveal the functioning of the model that they inherited—a model that conditions today's racism.

Presuppositions govern the interpretations of events and ultimately the range of culturally acceptable political action. The presupposition of gradation set in place the notion that difference means difference in value on a vertical scale of values. It yielded the statement by Nott and Gliddon that "no two distinctly-marked races can dwell together on equal terms" (Nott and Gliddon 79). And it influenced theories of evolution. In our time, it yielded the IQ test, as Stephen Jay Gould has shown in *The Mismeasure of Man*; the IQ test ranks human intelligence on a unilinear scale. The presupposition of a spirit/matter distinction set in place the notion that those beings who can be characterized as least occupied with satisfying immediate material needs rank highest, because they are least animal-like. Of course, the civilizations with the greatest material wealth, much of which they had acquired through conquest, colonization, and slavery, offered their elite the most leisure time for contemplation of truth and beauty; so their citizens appeared, in Gobineau's assessment, to be the most intelligent and the most spiritual. The presupposition of stasis—that nature's order is God-given, unchanging, eternal—made species, race, and rank appear permanent. The presupposition that reality is atomistic inclined ethnologists to look for absolute distinctions among the races. The presupposition of divine Creation gave rise to the question of whether members of the Negro race were descended from Adam.

❧ Darwinism

When Darwin discredited the typological species concept, he rendered obsolete the model of reality as static, atomistic, and dualistic. Ultimately, his theory replaced the concept of gradation in nature with that of ecosystem.

In the *Origin of Species* Darwin amassed enough evidence of evolution to convince the scientific community that the multitudinous species living in the present had descended, through a slow process of modification, from a few very different species in the remote past; that the mechanism for this evolution is *natural selection*[14] operating on populations of organisms; and that natural selection accounts for the adaptation of species to varying physical circumstances, such as climate, and the extinction of species unable to adapt. Nature's process for selection is blind competition. Darwin viewed *survival* in terms of reproductive success: Organisms within a species vary from each other, and those organisms best adapted to their environment are most likely to survive long enough to reproduce and thereby to transmit their advantageous traits to the next generation (Darwin, *Origin*, 1st ed. 62). *Variety* is natural, and *diversity* benefits the species: "the more diversified these descendants become, the better will be their chance of succeeding in the battle of life" (Darwin, *Origin*, 1st ed. 128).[15]

In *The Descent of Man* Darwin clarified his argument that "man must be included with other organic beings in any general conclusion respecting his manner of appearance on this earth" (*Descent* 1: 1).

Although he introduced a holistic model of reality with his depiction of nature as a "tangled bank,"[16] Darwin transmitted in his rhetoric the idea of a ladder of progress. For example:

> It may be said that natural selection is daily and hourly scrutinising, throughout the world, every variation, even the slightest; rejecting that which is bad, preserving and adding up all that is good; silently and insensibly working, whenever and wherever opportunity offers, at the improvement of each organic being in relation to its organic and inorganic conditions of life. We see nothing of these slow changes in progress, until the hand of time has marked the long lapse of ages. (Darwin, *Origin*, 1st ed. 84)

> It is apparently a truer and more cheerful view that progress has been much more general than retrogression; that man has risen, though by slow and interrupted steps, from a lowly condition to the highest standard as yet attained by him in knowledge, morals, and religion. (Darwin, *Descent* 1: 184)

By associating morality with human reason (Darwin, *Descent* 2: 394),[17] Darwin superimposed a hierarchy of goodness upon the scale of civilization. Ironically, his fully materialist, temporal explanation for human origins followed the medieval Christian model, Dante's model, in which an individual's holiness was measured by the dominance of spiritual concerns over material or instinctual desires. In Darwin's scheme, the arts signified a population's state of evolutionary progress.

That hierarchical model governed Darwin's understanding of the races and the sexes. For Darwin, as well as for Gobineau, nature and culture served as the poles of a scale of ascent. Gobineau and most of the ethnologists of his age considered the black race less intelligent than the white, less civilized, more sensual, more oriented toward sexual gratification, and therefore closer to nature. On a scale of primitive-to-civilized, they put Aryans at the top for their degree of culture. Darwin did the same, though with the argument that natural selection, rather than God, determined the ranking.

> At some future period, not very distant as measured by centuries, the civilised races of man will almost certainly exterminate and replace throughout the world the savage races. . . . The break will then be rendered wider, for it will intervene between man in a more civilised state, as we may hope, than the Caucasian, and some ape as low as a baboon, instead of as at present between the negro or Australian and the gorilla. (Darwin, *Descent* 1: 201)[18]

Darwin also attributed to evolution the intellectual differences he perceived between the sexes. These differences, he said, had developed at an early stage of human evolution, when males more than females had to be good at observation, reason, invention, and imagination to avoid or attack enemies, to capture wild animals, and to fashion weapons. Natural selection had transmitted the advantageous characteristics to male offspring (*Descent* 2: 328). Consequently, "Man is more courageous, pugnacious, and energetic than woman, and has a more inventive genius" (Darwin, *Descent* 2: 316).

> It is generally admitted that with woman the powers of intuition, of rapid perception, and perhaps of imitation, are more strongly marked than in man; but some, at least, of these faculties are characteristic of the lower races, and therefore of a past and lower state of civilisation.
>
> The chief distinction in the intellectual powers of the two sexes is shewn by man attaining to a higher eminence, in whatever he takes up, than woman can attain—whether requiring deep thought, reason, or imagination, or merely the use of the senses and hands. If two lists were made of the most eminent men and women in poetry, painting, sculpture, music,—comprising composition and performance, history, science, and philosophy, with half-a-dozen names under each subject, the two lists would not bear comparison. (Darwin, *Descent* 2: 326–327).

With his statement that women's powers of intuition, rapid perception, and imitation "are characteristic of the lower races, and therefore of a past and lower state of civilisation," Darwin linked women with "the lower races." One might wonder, in light of his equation of intellect with morality, whether Darwin supposed women to be less morally sensitive than men.

Although he discredited the spirit/matter dualism in biology by demonstrating that natural processes alone could bring about evolutionary change, Darwin thus adhered to it in his culture/nature hierarchy. In Darwin's argument we see that racism and sexism have the same philosophical foundation: a dualism of culture and nature, predicated on the dualism of spirit and matter, which privileges white over colored and male over female. Colored is closer to nature than white; woman is closer to nature than man. With the assumption that whites and males are intellectually superior to nonwhites and females, Western societies established laws and customs that perpetuated an inequality of educational opportunity and thereby reinforced public perception that the culturally derived vertical order was natural.

What interests us about these passages from Darwin's *Descent of Man, and Selection in Relation to Sex* is not their revelation that the great naturalist was a racist and a sexist but instead their indication of the power and persuasiveness of the vertical model. Certainly, Darwin was perceptive, open-minded, and relentlessly honest in his pursuit of truth. Yet he was a European man of his times, despite his revolutionary understanding of nature; he rid himself of some of the theological and scientific notions he had inherited, but he largely retained his society's system of values. Within that system man's inherent superiority to woman seemed verified by the intellectual, financial, artistic, military, and physical activities in which men excelled more than women. And white Europeans' superiority to people of color around the world, in an empire where the sun never set, seemed demonstrated by their conquests. Darwin and his fellow Victorians took a civilized nation's imperialistic success, which Darwin attributed to its arts (Darwin, *Descent* 1: 169), as an index to the intelligence of its citizens and to their natural superiority over the citizens of barbarous nations.

From our viewpoint Darwin was mistaken here; he was confusing culture with nature. Paradoxically, even as he repudiated the concept of species types, he retained a belief in the races' and the sexes' "typical" characteristics. Inheriting his society's ideology of individualism, Darwin ignored how customs, laws, and language positioned particular individuals or groups to do those things that were considered the mark of civilization. And although he believed that the rational self developed as a result of natural processes alone, his inattention to the effect of laws and customs on individuals, in his description of racial and sexual characteristics, shows a residual dualism: the presupposition that one's intellectual life was separable from one's material circumstances.

In the long run, however, Darwin's theory of natural selection undermined the spirit/matter dualism, the concept of types, and the vertical order in which differences mean differences in rank. In Darwin's model difference means diversity, which occurs naturally. With the *Origin* Darwin revolutionized the study of living forms by replacing typological thinking with population thinking. If *species* do not represent eternal types, if they in fact are mutable, then they are only categories of organisms—that is, *populations*—to be defined statistically. Accordingly, there is no single, correct appearance for an organism, only a population average and variance. There is no ideal structure, no ideal mode of behavior, only different strategies for adaptation to changing environmental conditions. There is no fixed, or God-ordained, relationship of organisms to each other, no eternal order. Nature is continuously changing. Species develop in geological time, become extinct, and are replaced by others. Humans are one such species.

Thinkers on both the left and the right of the political spectrum translated Darwin's ideas into social theory. Karl Marx, who with Friedrich Engels had published the *Communist Manifesto* in 1848, liked the *Origin* for its materialist conception of history.[19] For Marx, Darwin's dismissal of the design argument represented a challenge to the established social hierarchy, which was held in place by the church as much as by the state. In exposing as a myth the concept of a permanent order of nature, in which organisms manifested eternal types and occupied their God-given, permanent niches on the scale of ascent, Darwinian theory dissolved the theological foundation for the class system. That is why many members of England's privileged upper class, who associated Darwin's ideas with the atheistic materialism of the French Revolution, feared Darwinism. They feared an ideology that, in their view, suggested the possibility of social mobility through individual effort.

However, it was precisely this latter interpretation of Darwinism that others on the right approved, for they believed that the biological principle of natural selection ratified the social inequalities they observed. Supporters of laissez-faire capitalism, the "Social Darwinists" took as their rallying cry the phrase "survival of the fittest," which the English philosopher Herbert Spencer had coined and Darwin had adopted in the later editions of the *Origin*.[20] According to Social Darwinism, those who had made it to the top of the social ladder had been naturally selected for their position; they were the fittest, the best, the survivors in the competition for wealth. Spencer, like Thomas Malthus before him, went as far as to oppose state assistance to the poor, since that would enable them to survive and proliferate: The state should not interfere with the forces of nature. Darwin had applied Malthus's social theory to nature. Now Spencer and such American disciples as the oil baron John D. Rockefeller and the industrialist Andrew Carnegie were applying Darwin's evolutionism to society.

In "The Gospel of Wealth," which he first published in the *North American Review* in 1899, Carnegie lauded competition as nature's means of "advancing" human society, for although the law might be hard on some individuals, "it is best for the race, because it insures survival of the fittest in every department" (Carnegie 16). He welcomed, "as conditions to which we must accommodate ourselves," social inequality, the concentration of business in the hands of a few, and the law of competition, for being "essential to the future progress of the race" (Carnegie 16–17). Carnegie's theory was a kind of temporalized scale of ascent, in which the wealthiest occupied the position of the most highly evolved, the most distant from their primitive origins: "The contrast between the palace of the millionaire and the cottage of the laborer with us to-day measures the change which has come with civilization" (Carnegie 14).[21] For Carnegie, Darwinism gave biological support not to the doctrine of communism, as Marx had thought, but to the doctrine of individualism.[22] Individualism, private property, the accumulation of wealth, and competition have been the soil, wrote Carnegie, in which society "has produced the best fruit" (Carnegie 19).

In Social Darwinism we see the reception of Darwin's theory of populations by a society whose model of order was a hierarchy. Those at the bottom of the social scale, those workers who earned little in the factories and the mines, made possible the accumulation of wealth by their employers, who, according to this doctrine, returned it to society in the form of "the refinements of civilization." In Carnegie's gospel, "It is well, nay, essential, for the progress of the race that the houses of some should be homes for all that is highest and best in literature and the arts, and for all the refinements of civilization, rather than that none should be so" (Carnegie 15). With the presupposition that difference meant difference in rank, the Social Darwinists, who were themselves near the top of the social and economic scale, interpreted the principle of natural selection operating on diversity to explain the great differences in fortune between the indigent and the wealthy. They took Darwin's "laws of nature" to justify their own financial success, their own enviable position on the ladder.

The conflicting interpretations of Darwinian theory with respect to the individual's place in nature brought about intense political debate. In the nineteenth century antievolutionists had attacked Darwin for not subscribing to the sacredness of the individual human being, for viewing nature as a community of organisms that included humans; they considered the evolutionists left-wing and dangerous to society's stability. At the turn of the century the right-wing Social Darwinists understood Darwin to support individualism, in contrast with communism, which emphasized the community over the individual. Although they embraced the theory the antievolutionists despised, the Social Darwinists shared with the antievolutionists a privileging of the individual over the community. An atomistic economic philosophy, deeply embedded in Western individualism, generated opposition to any system of thought that focused on the community.

In 1902, Petr Kropotkin, a Russian prince-turned-anarchist, challenged Darwin's individualist description of nature in a book called *Mutual Aid: A Factor of Evolution*. Believing nature to be characterized more by cooperation than by competition, Kropotkin questioned Darwin's idea of intraspecies competition, which he said had become an "article of faith with most Darwinists," more so, actually, than with Darwin himself, whom he admired. With scores of examples to show that the "fittest" in nature were not those continually at war with each other but rather those who had acquired habits of "mutual aid," Kropotkin argued that mutual aid was as much a natural law of animal life as mutual contest. Moreover, since mutual support enabled animals not only to survive but to leave progeny, natural selection favored the formation of sociability. Kropotkin credited Darwin's *Descent of Man* with inspiring his own exploration of mutual aid.[23] And he criticized bitterly the appropriation of Darwin's ideas by a society obsessed with the individual.

And while in a savage land, among the Hottentots, it would be scandalous to eat without having loudly called out thrice whether there is not somebody wanting to share the food, all that a respectable citizen has to do now is to pay the poor tax and let the starving starve. The result is, that the theory which maintains that men can, and must, seek their own happiness in a disregard of other people's wants is now triumphant all round—in law, in science, in religion. It is the religion of the day, and to doubt of its efficacy is to be a dangerous Utopian. Science loudly proclaims that the struggle of each against all is the leading principle of nature, and of human societies as well. To that struggle Biology ascribes the progressive evolution of the animal world. History takes the same line of argument; and political economists, in their naive ignorance, trace all progress of modern industry and machinery to the "wonderful" effects of the same principle. The very religion of the pulpit is a religion of individualism, slightly mitigated by more or less charitable relations to one's neighbours, chiefly on Sundays. (Kropotkin 228)

The relatively new discipline of ecology has answered Kropotkin's plea for attention to mutual aid in its study of *biotic communities*, which include all of the populations of organisms in a particular area; of *ecosystems*, the biotic and abiotic components of a given area considered as a whole; and of the *biosphere*, the whole of the earth's ecosystems. It was Sir Arthur Tansley, a founder of the British Ecological Society, the world's first, who coined the word *ecosystem* in 1935 to describe the mutual dependence not only of animals on plants but of plants on animals and their interaction with the nonliving world (Odum 38). Ecologists now recognize the interaction of the biosphere with the *lithosphere*, the rocks, sediments, mantle, and core of the earth; the *hydrosphere*, surface and ground water; and the *atmosphere* (Odum 27–28). The model of individual struggle, which Kropotkin discerned in Darwinism, has been complemented, at least in ecology, with the model of cooperation: the theory that cooperation benefits individuals in long-term interactions more than does competition, which benefits individuals primarily in the short run. A theory of *coevolution*, suggested first by Darwin and developed in detail in 1965 by Paul Ehrlich and Peter Raven, explains the evolution of species in relation to each other.

In the "New Synthesis" reached by evolutionary geneticists in the late 1930s and early 1940s, it is the population, or the reproductive community, that receives attention. *Species* is now defined, in Ernst Mayr's words, as "a genetic unit consisting of a large, intercommunicating gene pool, whereas the individual is merely a temporary vessel holding a small portion of the contents of the gene pool for a short period of time." There is no species "essence" because *genotypes* vary from organism to organism within a group of individuals, who may in fact have similar *phenotypes* (that is, may resemble each other). A *race* is simply a population of individual organisms that differs noticeably, that is, "on sight," from other populations of the same species. Races overlap and evolve. There is no racial ideal. There is no stasis. There is no rank order. Chance can produce genetic variation. Diversity is natural, as well as beneficial to an ecosystem's stability.[24]

Paradoxically, "by emphasizing that each individual is uniquely different from every other one, the students of diversity have focused attention on the importance of the individual" (Mayr, *Evolution* 414), while simultaneously viewing the individual as part of a population. In this respect, the holistic model abandons the dilemma given by dualism of attending either to the individual or to the community; it is the interaction of individuals with each other in a community that defines the whole.

☙ The Best Known and Thought

While a holistic model of nature was moving into place in the sciences during the first half of the twentieth century, dualism continued to govern the humanities. Having inherited in the West's spirit/matter dichotomy a view that science described only the material aspects of reality, whereas literature expressed the human spirit, many humanists developed a contempt for— and an ignorance of—scientific explanations of the world.[25] Largely unaware of the very different understanding of reality that biologists and physicists had developed, literature professors transmitted to their students the traditional values of the writers of the past. And their disconnection of art from politics rendered impotent in the classroom any literature that called for fundamental social change.

The academic discipline of literary study obtained many of its principles from Matthew Arnold. Arnold's project for "criticism"—"to learn and propagate the best that is known and thought in the world" (Arnold 3: 283)—was based upon the same presuppositions that had given rise to the typological species concept and the ranking of the races: that values were intrinsic and permanent; that the order of things was hierarchical; and that observers could intellectually separate themselves from the world they observed. Truth could be known, and the best could be determined. Criticism proved its disinterestedness, Arnold wrote, by leaving alone "all questions of practical consequences and applications" (Arnold 3: 270). Because spirit transcended matter, knowledge was independent of politics, and literature was distinguishable from practical discourse.

Arnold's concept of humane letters was actually rather broad.[26] Nevertheless, his identification of *culture* with knowledge of the best known and thought in the world rested squarely on the spirit/matter dualism. "Culture," wrote Arnold, gave "sweetness and light," and "he who works for sweetness and light, works to make reason and the will of God prevail" (Arnold 5: 112). He called culture a mainstay of authority against anarchy: In a world of social flux, culture provided "right reason" (Arnold 5: 126). Furthermore, culture kept individuals from being "Philistines," concerned only with material wealth; wealth was machinery (Arnold 5: 97).

Arnold thus translated the opposition of spirit to matter into the oppositions of culture to Philistinism, authority to anarchy, knowledge to politics, and "sweetness and light" to, presumably, the darkness of ignorance, in which the unlettered, vulgar masses dwelled. By associating culture with "reason and the will of God" and by distinguishing it from materialistic endeavors, Arnold encouraged in generations of literary scholars a disdain for persons in science, business, and politics. By associating culture with Western civilization alone, he contributed to the dualism of Western and non-Western that was not to be challenged until the late twentieth century, when the curriculum debate in American colleges and universities laid bare the ideological content of the humanities.[27]

Americans received Arnold's ideas largely through the modernist poetry and criticism of T. S. Eliot. For Eliot, technology turned individuals into automatons, unintelligent, unmannered, unhappy, and incapable of appreciating the best known and thought in the world. Eliot's vision of a waste land whose bored inhabitants did not share values, purposes, ideals, or convictions, who did not share religious experience, who did not form a community, who lacked the spiritual energy that would make them fully human, became, for students of twentieth-century literature, an appropriate interpretation of modernity. The canonization of Eliot's poetry meant the canonization of his representation of reality.

Eliot's legacy consisted of a profound political conservatism formulated first in aesthetically avant-garde poetry and later in essays. In 1949, the year after he won the Nobel Prize, he published *Notes towards the Definition of Culture*, in which he urged the maintaining of a class society. Although he did not locate culture in the privileged classes alone, since culture encompassed such diverse accomplishments as urbanity, learning, philosophy, and the arts, all found "in the pattern of the society as a whole" (Eliot, *Notes* 21), Eliot held the upper classes responsible for the preservation and transmission of culture. He opposed the "dogma of equal opportunity" because it would disorganize society "by substituting for [hereditary] classes, elites of brains" (Eliot, *Notes* 103).[28] An educational system oriented toward equal opportunity would identify education with worldly success, to the end of disintegrating the classes and inspiring envy; envy would in turn fuel the "flame of 'equal opportunity'" (Eliot *Notes* 107). Moreover, the education of too many individuals would result in a lowering of standards. The purpose of education should be "to preserve the class and to select the elite"—but only a few "brains" from the nonpriviliged classes, supposedly, should be selected (Eliot, *Notes* 103).

Eliot's distaste for democracy was not unusual among the Anglo-American literary intelligentsia during the first half of this century. Henry James had written of democracy in 1908: "Vulgarity enthroned and institutionalised, elbowing everything superior from the highway; this, they tell us, is our irremedial destiny" (quoted in Harrison 26). Eliot's fellow poets Ezra Pound, William Butler Yeats, and Wyndham Lewis all feared the rise of what F. R. Leavis called "mass culture" (Leavis 169). Pound and Lewis supported fascism. Eliot, who was anti-Semitic as well as antidemocratic, used Jews in his poetry to symbolize moneymaking, which he associated with the degeneration of civilization.[29] What these writers wished to preserve was an aristocratic tradition that fostered great art, a stable social hierarchy. Democratic education, predicted Eliot, would destroy "our ancient edifices to make ready the ground upon which the barbarian nomads of the future will encamp in their mechanised caravans" (Eliot, *Notes* 111).

From the 1930s through the 1950s, literary study in the United States was dominated by the so-called New Critics, who aimed to focus attention on literature's purely aesthetic nature. Influenced by Eliot's atomistic concept of "tradition" as a set of literary "monuments," which Eliot had expounded in his 1917 essay "Tradition and the Individual Talent" (Eliot, "Tradition" 49–50), Cleanth Brooks and Robert Penn Warren called for a reorientation in the teaching of literature to "the poem in itself." In *Understanding Poetry*, which effectively installed New Criticism in the college classroom, Brooks and Warren explained: "Though one may consider a poem as an instance of historical or ethical documentation, the poem in itself, if literature is to be studied as literature, remains finally the object for study" (Brooks and Warren iv). Privileging aesthetically complex poetry that rewarded close reading without regard to its social context, Brooks and Warren omitted from their volume many poems that had been included in other major poetry anthologies of the early twentieth century, poems by the black poets James Weldon Johnson, Paul Laurence Dunbar, Claude McKay, Jean Toomer, Langston Hughes, and Countee Cullen, and poems from such categories as American Indian poetry, Negro spirituals, and backwoods ballads (Craige 80, 139–140).

The New Criticism conveyed certain attitudes that can be traced back to a notion of Aristotle's: that poetry was "higher" and more philosophical than history because poetry expressed the universal and history the particular. The

New Critics translated the Aristotelian dichotomy into a distinction between the experience of an individual and the experience of a collective. They focused on the individual condition rather than on the social condition in the belief that certain supposedly universal human experiences transcended particular social circumstances; and they ranked higher the literary works that seemed to embody "universal values" than those that articulated a group's particular circumstances. As we can see now, those in the positions of power to determine which texts expressed universal values assumed their own values to be universally held, or held at least by right-thinking and sensitive people. They discounted the opinions of the masses: If a text appealed to the masses, it was obviously not literarily excellent.

The definition of literature as transcendent to politics and to the particular removed from the range of most students the poems, novels, and plays that might affect their political outlook. The many imaginative works written to arouse interest in controversial political issues or to call attention to social injustices, the many texts by women and people of color that illuminated particular social conditions, the conditions of the powerless, were disregarded.[30] They were not classified among "the best" and therefore were not taught. Few of the socially engaged poems published during the 1920s and 1930s in such journals as *The Masses, Liberator, The New Masses, Dynamo, The Rebel Poet, The Latin Quarterly, Challenge, Morada, Poetry, Midwest, The New Quarterly, The Anvil, New Anvil,* and *Partisan Review* made their way into college textbook anthologies (Nelson 101), in part because they did not foreground language and technique the way modernist poetry did, and in part because they served overtly political purposes. They did not seem "literary" to the New Critics, who judged politically motivated works of the left, or works that articulated social oppression, to be "propaganda."

Because the New Critical anthologies were widely adopted, even such prominent leftist thinkers as Malcolm Cowley, Alfred Kazin, and Irving Howe, whose books of criticism became standard reading for graduate students of English, exerted relatively little influence on undergraduates. The New Critical canon became "the canon"—taken to be "the best that is known and thought in the world."

In classifying Western texts alone in the category of "the best," New Critics promoted belief in the superiority of the West over the rest of the world. With standards of literary excellence based on Western "masterpieces," Americans were not inclined to view non-Western texts, particularly those serving different ideological purposes, as literature. Since, in the hierarchical model, artistic accomplishments indicated degree of civilization and hence rank, Americans educated in the humanities inherited with that model a greater respect for the colonizing nations than for the colonized, a higher esteem for the white race than for the colored races, and a greater admiration of men's abilities than of women's. Contributions to "culture" seemed to come from the imperialist nations, the white race, and men.

The discipline of literary study, as it matured under the influence of Arnold, Eliot, and the New Critics, thus reinforced the political status quo. In the dualist model in which aesthetic values were presumed to be independent of politics, literature professors devoted themselves to the literary; they were philosophically conditioned to regard society's ills as irrelevant to art and irrelevant to their scholarship.

The category of "the best that is known and thought in the world" thus rests upon racism, imperialism, and prejudice based on sex and class. It developed out of the vertical conceptualization of reality, and it has perpetuated it. At the end of the twentieth century the intense debate over undergraduate education is a sign that this model is in crisis.

In defending the teaching of "the best," traditionalists are really defending their own long-standing social order. They naturally feel threatened by those who advocate an appreciation of cultural diversity. For the traditionalists, who see difference as inequality, the appreciation of diversity means egalitarianism and egalitarianism means the advancement of the inferior. They recognize the cultural holists' project to integrate the curriculum as a sign of social revolution.

All this pitting of sex against sex, of quality against quality; all this claiming of superiority and imputing of inferiority, belong to the private-school stage of human existence where there are "sides," and it is necessary for one side to beat another side, and of the utmost importance to walk up to a platform and receive from the hands of the Headmaster himself a highly ornamental pot.
—*Virginia Woolf,* A Room of One's Own, *1929*

The Movement does not seek to liberate Negroes at the expense of the humiliation and enslavement of whites. It seeks no victory over anyone. It seeks to liberate American society and to share in the self-liberation of all people.
—*Martin Luther King,* Nobel Lecture, *1964*

2 ❧ Equal Rights

In 1928, having acquired fame as the author of *Mrs. Dalloway, To the Lighthouse,* and *Orlando,* the English novelist Virginia Woolf was invited to speak to several women's clubs on the subject of "women and fiction." Little did her audience realize then how important those talks were to become. With the publication the following year of *A Room of One's Own,* an expansion of the lectures, Woolf initiated the feminist analysis of aesthetics that became a critique of the traditional undergraduate curriculum.

Western aesthetics at the time Woolf gave her lectures rested upon the dualist assumption that the aesthetic transcended the political. According to the New Critics, individual artists could ignore their particular material circumstances—that is, the circumstances of sex, class, and race—to express universal concerns. If they did not, they were not writing "literature." With the observation that most of the great English writers of the nineteenth century were "University men," and fairly well-to-do, Woolf asked, "What conditions are necessary for the creation of works of art?" (Woolf 25). Why did men alone write "literature"? She concluded that in order to write one needed education, money, and "a room of one's own," which few women had enjoyed. "Intellectual freedom depends upon material things. Poetry depends upon intellectual freedom. And women have always been poor, not for two hundred years merely, but from the beginning of time" (Woolf 112).

In calling attention to the social impediments to a woman's participation in the culture's intellectual discourse, Woolf exposed the political infrastructure of the category of "the best that is known and thought in the world." Her argument that society structures consciousness challenged the prevailing Anglo-American belief in the relative autonomy of the individual, and her mockery of competition to determine "the best" challenged the vertical conceptual model that made for ranking. That model could be likened to a "zero-sum game," in which one's success depends upon one's opponent's failure (Allman 27).

Martin Luther King, as leader of the civil rights movement in the United States, also recognized oppression as an effect of the vertical model in which success is defined by rank on a scale of well-being and the well-being of one individual or group is achieved at the expense of another. In King's vision, the old order would eventually be replaced by a new order, not characterized by zero-sum thinking, in which the liberation of the oppressed, whom he represented, would not require the humiliation and enslavement of the former oppressors. He had rejected violence, he said in accepting the 1964 Nobel Prize for Peace, because violence "seeks to humiliate the opponent rather than win his understanding: it seeks to annihilate rather than convert" (King, *Nobel Lecture* 9).

Nevertheless, King continued to argue, human dignity required economic justice: Intellectual freedom depended upon material things. The blacks would not be intellectually free until they were no longer economically oppressed. In one speech after another King pointed out that economic injustice exacerbated racial prejudice, just as racial prejudice exacerbated economic injustice. Critical of an economic order that relegated some members of society to poverty, he said, "an edifice which produces beggars needs restructuring" (King, *Testament* 250).

In the 1960s, leaders of both the civil rights movement and the women's movement called for a system in which individuals would be judged, as in King's dream, not "by the color of their skin but by the content of their character" (King, *Testament* 219), not by their sex but by their capability. They called for a legislated equality of opportunity and a prohibition of institutional racial and sexual oppression. King's plea that blacks not distrust all whites, because "many of our white brothers . . . have come to realize that their destiny is tied up with our destiny and . . . that their freedom is inextricably bound to our freedom" (King, *Testament* 218), heralds a model of cooperation rather than one of competition, a holistic model in which the recognition of the interdependence of all human beings should bring an appreciation of diversity and a respect for differences. Ideally, it should bring—in time—an end to the "claiming of superiority and imputing of inferiority."

Both sexism and racism are predicated upon a confusion between the natural and the cultural from which we humans can never fully escape, the confusion between what is given by nature and what we are predisposed by the structure of our thinking to see. In recent years advocates of sexual and racial equality of opportunity have come to believe that much of what was once thought "natural" in gender and racial differences is actually "cultural."

Darwin revolutionized biology when he rejected the typological species concept in favor of the nondualistic population concept, but he expressed his society's traditional views when he assumed, on the basis of their artistic and intellectual accomplishments, that men were more intelligent than women and that whites were more intelligent than blacks. In his mind, he was not being inconsistent, for he ascribed to natural causes the perceived sexual and racial intellectual inequalities. For Darwin, as for many nineteenth-century ethnologists, biological evolution produced cultural differences; degree of culture indicated rank on an evolutionary scale. From the viewpoint of twentieth-century social egalitarians, however, cultural evolution produced the intellectual differences that have been considered biological. Like Darwin, most advocates for sexual and racial social equality today reject the notion of an eternal order governing social interaction in the world, but unlike Darwin they do not attribute intellectual and artistic achievement to sexual or racial differences.

The dualism rooted in the Western construction of reality took a variety of forms. Darwin fought the dualism of spirit and matter as a dualism of Platonic types and their appearances in the natural world; he explained the origin of species in terms of natural causality, and he went on to explain the growth of culture materialistically. His theory of natural selection, when widely accepted, exposed the cultural basis for the concept of species' fixity. A hundred years later the advocates of sexual and racial equality are fighting the dualism of spirit and matter as a dualism of intellectual achievement and economic circumstances, explaining intellectual achievement, as well as racial prejudices, in terms of economic and legal relationships. Their theory exposes the cultural basis for Darwin's views of gender and racial characteristics.

Thus, although we can say that both Darwin and the twentieth-century advocates for equal rights have abandoned the spirit/matter dualism, the rights advocates are engaged in a different battle from Darwin's. In the argument that society is morally obligated to attempt to provide equal educational and economic opportunity to its citizens, they are combatting the individualism that presupposed the independence of individuals' intellectual and moral life from material circumstances. They are also rejecting the concept of social order as naturally vertical, because that presumption served to legitimate oppression. They are cultural holists, whose inclusivism represents an understanding of nature in which human society may be conceived not as a ladder, not even as a ladder laid down, but as a web of men and women of various colors and beliefs whose well-being is a responsibility of the whole.

🕭 Education for Women

The political activists engaged in the recent legal struggles for equal opportunity are now pointing to the ways the dualist conceptual model has institutionalized social injustices. The culture/nature dichotomy inspired the opinion that women were closer to nature than men and that blacks were closer to nature than whites. Since culture was privileged over nature, the more "natural" were considered innately inferior to the more "cultured." They were consequently deprived of educational and economic opportunities to become "cultured."

Late-nineteenth-century essays on women's education provide us with some insight into how the traditional understanding of racial and sexual differences that derived from laws and customs in turn affected laws and customs. A hundred years ago the discussion of whether women should be allowed higher education revolved not around equal rights but around perceived psychological and physiological capabilities. Most of those writing on the subject assumed that men excelled "in judgment, women in common sense" (W. K. Brooks 155), and that, because a woman's "opinions are formed by her feelings rather than by the operations of reason" (A. H. Bennett 524), women would not benefit from intellectual study. According to the physician A. Hughes Bennett, women, unlike men,

> can not fix the attention long and deeply, or persevere in overcoming obstructions, and they feel no pleasure in habits of profound meditation. They therefore remain with their acquired superficial knowledge, pass

rapidly from one thing to another, and there only rest in their minds certain crude and incomplete notions, with which they are quite satisfied, and of which they make the most, but which in consequence lead to false and illogical conclusions. (A. H. Bennett 524)

Here the culture/nature dualism is expressed as a distinction between reason and emotion, between judgment or abstract thought and common sense. It is also implicit in Bennett's failure to consider that education might inspire "habits of profound meditation," might offer women more than "superficial knowledge," and might change women's behavior. Woolf was to ask how women, particularly those responsible for a household, could ever find the time to fix their attention on an abstract idea. We might ask whether uneducated men, such as those of the lower classes who had not the wealth to pursue higher learning, themselves acquired more than "crude and incomplete" notions of things.

In a two-part essay published in the *Popular Science Monthly* in 1883 and 1884, T. S. Clouston, M.D., explained why women should not be permitted to stimulate the growth of their intellect at the expense of their bodily health. Since "a law of Nature" established limits to any individual's energy, such that its use for one activity meant its unavailability for another, Clouston recommended against women's attempting mental work. If during her adolescence a woman spent her energy acquiring "book-knowledge," she would never fully develop her feminine nature and would remain for the rest of her life "an imperfect organism" (Clouston 223). But more was at stake than her personal existence:

This is a poor lookout for the individual; but when motherhood comes, and sound minds in sound bodies have to be transmitted to posterity, how is it to be then with the future race? This aspect of the question of female education during the period of adolescence is of absolutely primary importance to the world. (Clouston 223)

Women's health was therefore more critical than men's:

The cheerfulness and vivacity that are [women's] special characteristic, seem to exist not for themselves alone, but for their families as well, and those are, generally speaking, wanting if the health is bad. Woman is gifted with the power not only of bearing her own share of ills, but of helping to bear those of others. She can't do so in the same degree if she is not in health. (Clouston 329)

On the culture/nature continuum, not only were women "naturally" closer to the nature pole than were civilized men, but the future of the human race required women to retain that position, Clouston was arguing. "There is no time or place of organic repentance provided by Nature for the sins of the schoolmaster" (Clouston 223). Civilized men were obliged to cultivate their minds; according to this medical "conservation-of-energy" theory, they were not to let excessive sexual activity jeopardize their intellectual life (Ehrenreich and English 27).

Implicit in the discussion over women and higher education, much of which took place on the pages of *Popular Science Monthly*, was a double bind for women. This was the logic: Because women were intellectually inferior to men, they were incapable of benefiting as fully as men from higher education. Therefore, instead of futilely attempting intellectual work, they should develop for the benefit of their families and of the human race their natural talents of maternal affection, instinctual empathy, intuitiveness, common sense, and cheerfulness. They should attend to their bodies, not their minds.[1]

Women were thus supposed to develop the qualities that made them natural, and therefore inferior to men, whereas men were supposed to develop the qualities that distinguished them from nature and made them superior to women. In short, women were supposed to aspire to a status of intellectual inferiority to men; they demonstrated virtue in being satisfied with their natural rank. Higher education enabled the society's privileged men—that is, those whose material circumstances gave them the intellectual freedom to study the laws of nature and to learn of the best thought and written—to maintain their status of intellectual superiority.

In *A Room of One's Own* Woolf imagined that Shakespeare had a sister named Judith, equally talented, equally driven to write plays. But, in contrast with her brother, Judith received no education in grammar, logic, or the works of Ovid, Virgil, and Horace; her fate was to be betrothed to the son of a neighboring wool stapler. In rebellion against her parents' plans for her, she ran away to London, where she hung around the theater, hoping to be involved in its activities. But there she was told that the theater had no place for women. After roaming the streets hungry, with no way to earn an honest living, Judith took up with an actor-manager, became pregnant, and in despair committed suicide. Woolf concluded the sad tale by saying that no woman born in Shakespeare's day could have had Shakespeare's genius, for without some education, opportunity, and intellectual freedom, a woman with such a great gift in the sixteenth century "would certainly have gone crazed, shot herself, or ended her days in some lonely cottage outside the village, half witch, half wizard, feared and mocked at" (Woolf 51).

Woolf used Shakespeare's sister as a metaphor for women of her own day, who were prohibited from attending the great universities, who were consequently denied the opportunity to use the great universities' libraries, who—if they came from well-to-do families—could attend women's colleges but were generally discouraged from pursuing a career. Society's laws and customs enforced an intellectual inequality between the sexes.

❧ Racial Integration

In the 1960s and 1970s civil rights activists and feminists were often accused of wishing to invert the established social order. If feminists did not believe men to be superior to women, the argument went, then they must believe women superior to men. If blacks objected to their inferior status, then they obviously wanted to dominate. Even the seemingly fair and nonhierarchical principle of "equal pay for equal work" was threatening; to some it meant that those who deserved less because they were worth less would have to be treated the same as those who by nature deserved more. In the zero-sum model an increase in legal rights, prestige, power, or standard of living of people at the bottom of the ladder means a decrease in legal rights, prestige, power, or standard of living of people at the top. Those who conceive of order as vertical, in which difference signifies difference in rank, understand any change in social or economic relationships either among the races or between the sexes to be a change in the rank order. A change in the rank order is the definition of revolution, for it means a redistribution of resources. That is why J. Edgar Hoover in 1958 initiated an FBI investigation of King and his associates (Powers 369) and in 1971 began assembling files on the feminist movement (Albert and Albert 51).

In the 1963 campaign for racial justice in Birmingham, Alabama, where King led the Southern Christian Leadership Conference (SCLC) in nonviolent direct action to integrate public facilities,[2] we can see the conflict between the vertical model of social order and the holistic. There King's goal was not a reversal of the hierarchy of privilege but rather an abandonment of it; and his tactic was not violent overthrow but rather militant *nonviolence*, designed to expose institutional injustice by provoking racists to violence against nonviolent demonstrators exercising their civil rights.[3] This strategy for social change comes out of a nonoppressive model for social interaction.

Institutional injustice, though it may masquerade as peace, is tacitly violent, King argued. In his "Letter from Birmingham Jail," a reply to eight "liberal" Alabama clergymen who had previously warned King that his nonviolent resistance would incite violence, King wrote: "You deplore the demonstrations taking place in Birmingham. But your statement, I am sorry to say, fails to express a similar concern for the conditions that brought about the demonstrations" (King, *Why We Can't Wait* 79). In other words, the system of segregation, based as it was on the presumed superiority of whites, did violence to blacks; it held blacks economically and socially at the bottom of the scale. As long as the blacks did not protest their low rank, the whites above them assumed that the community was at peace. But when the disadvantaged began disturbing the peace, demanding that they be given the rights the whites had always enjoyed, Bull Connor's police had to use force. The police used violence to keep the peace.

King used nonviolence to expose the violence inherent in the unjust system. It was a method and a philosophy, which he learned from Mohandas Gandhi, consistent with his desire for a nonviolent society. As King described it in his Nobel address,

> nonviolence in the civil rights struggle has meant not relying on arms and weapons of struggle. It has meant non-cooperation with customs and laws which are institutional aspects of a regime of discrimination and enslavement. It has meant direct participation of masses in protest, rather than reliance on indirect methods which frequently do not involve masses in action at all. (King, *Nobel Lecture* 8)

To use violence would have implied a desire simply to invert the established hierarchy, replacing white oppressors with black oppressors; and preserving the new hierarchy would have required the same kind of force that the segregationists had employed "to keep the Negro in his place." As surely as injustice begat violence, violence begat injustice. Violence as a military strategy was appropriate to maintain a vertical order, a zero-sum system of rights and benefits, the model of conquest and oppression. Militant nonviolence, whose purpose was to change people's minds, was appropriate to achieve a nonoppressive system.

Nonviolence as an alternative to violence for improving racial relations was only apparently passive. Nonviolent resisters, King had written in a 1957 essay published in *Christian Century*, objected as strongly to the particular "evil" they protested as did those who used violence. However, because the nonviolent resisters were actually fighting the institutions that perpetuated the evil, not the individuals caught by the institutions, they refrained from using physical violence against their opponents. They thereby refrained from doing violence to their own spirit. Nonviolence was impersonal—that is, nonindividualistic—in its assumption that human behavior is a function of social and economic conditions and that the character of the victimizers as well as the victimized is produced by social structures. Nonviolent resisters aimed not to defeat the opponent but to win the opponent's friendship and understanding and to change the structures that produced the hostility; they used boycotts and noncooperation as means to awaken moral shame, not as ends in themselves. The desired end, said King, was redemption and reconciliation. "To retaliate with hate and bitterness would do nothing but intensify the hate in the world" (King, *Testament* 7–8).

King's strategy of nonviolence worked well in the age of television, when coverage of police violence touched the consciences of voters across the country. It led to the passage of the Civil Rights Act of 1964 and, eventually, to a somewhat less racist society. However, as King recognized, racism was inextricably bound to economic oppression. Racial equality required economic justice.

In the middle and late sixties, King and the other advocates of nonviolence had increasing difficulty preventing the violence that arose from the desire for economic justice. After the summer of 1964, even the Student Nonviolent Coordinating Committee (SNCC), which had been founded upon principles adopted from the Gandhian independence movement and from the American traditions of pacifism and Christian idealism, began losing faith in the power of nonviolent protest to effect economic and political change (Carson 2–3).

Segregationists had legitimated their economic domination of blacks by ideology—by the theory of racial superiority—and they had enforced it by law and police action. With vicious circularity, their economic superiority had become an educational superiority, which in turn looked like an inherent intellectual superiority. The racial differences that had resulted from cultural processes, from slavery and economic oppression, appeared to have resulted from God's or nature's laws. That is why many white citizens found integration just as morally repugnant as black citizens found segregation. Because the poverty of the blacks affected their academic capabilities, their integration into previously all-white schools did in fact threaten the quality of the white children's education. From the viewpoint of many whites during the 1950s and 1960s, integration threatened "culture," the culture that the Western world had developed over centuries, the culture that distinguished humanity from nature. What it actually threatened was the position of socially privileged whites as guardians of "the best that is known and thought in the world."

However, as we have seen, a society that preserves "culture" by oppressing the "uncultured," those whom it has systematically deprived of educational and employment opportunities, is intrinsically unstable. In the dualist model such domination was not recognized as oppression; it was considered inherent in the triumph of civilization over nature. Furthermore, it was considered inherent in competition, deemed intellectually and technologically beneficial to a society: Competition put some at the top and others at the bottom. But in the holistic model such domination is understood to imperil the whole system, since the health of a society depends upon the health of the interdependent individuals composing it. Individuals are not healthy when angry, depressed, hungry, or homeless; nor can they contribute productively to the system.

🍂 Legislation

Today few critical thinkers ignore the effect of social organization on individuals. The ideology of individualism was predicated upon a belief in a rational self not fundamentally affected by the individual's material circumstances. Woolf and King presented an alternative, nondualist view, that "intellectual freedom depends upon material things." With the passage of the Civil Rights Act of 1964, Congress implicitly acknowledged that the ideas and attitudes of individuals are, to some extent, constituted by social structure. The Civil Rights Act served not only to guarantee civil rights to all citizens without regard to race, color, religion, sex, or national origin but also, by eliminating employment discrimination in industries affecting interstate commerce, to change existing relationships among citizens. This legislation, as well as subsequent interpretations of the Fourteenth Amendment, which grants all citizens "equal protection of the laws," offers evidence of an increasing egalitarianism in our legal system.

On July 2, 1964, President Johnson signed the Civil Rights Act into law. Its purpose was

To enforce the constitutional right to vote, to confer jurisdiction upon the district courts of the United States to provide injunctive relief against discrimination in public accommodations, to authorize the Attorney General to institute suits to protect constitutional rights in public facilities and public education, to extend the Commission on Civil Rights, to prevent discrimination in federally assisted programs, to establish a Commission on Equal Employment Opportunity, and for other purposes. (*Civil Rights Act* 103)

The spirit/matter dualism embedded in traditional American individualism supplied the arguments against the Civil Rights Act. For example, many conservatives objected to it on the grounds that "You can't legislate morality," that a society's moral values transcended its political structure, just as the individual's morality transcended his or her material circumstances. According to their reasoning, character was innate: If a white man had shown unethical prejudice against blacks before the bill was passed, he would continue to do so, regardless of the law; and if a black man had burglarized before the law enabled him to obtain employment, he would not be more honest afterward.

Others objected to the bill's passage for its promotion of a fully integrated society. Implicit in their fear of integration was the belief that the apparent intellectual inferiority of blacks to whites was natural and that equality of educational or occupational opportunity would not and could not affect that natural relationship: An individual's intelligence was independent of his or her material circumstances. Some extremists went so far as to put forth an argument common to the Reconstruction era: that integration would lead to intermarriage and thereby to the decline, through miscegenation, of American civilization, which they defined as white. We can trace this argument to the opinion that civilization has a genetic basis: that the genetically superior white race ranks higher than the black on the culture/nature continuum, that blacks are less evolutionarily advanced.

The Equal Rights Amendment (ERA), which passed the United States Senate in March of 1972 with a vote of 84 to 8 but failed to be ratified by the required thirty-eight states before the June 1982 deadline, also elicited opposition based on fear of structural change in our society. The amendment's opponents claimed that it would indeed affect a natural relationship, the traditional hierarchical relationship of man to woman; the ERA, they said, went against nature. ERA proponents believed that this hierarchical relationship, with its implication of man's innate intellectual superiority to woman, was not natural but cultural and that the legislation of equal rights would, in time, change the social perception that men were more intelligent than women.

The complete text of the proposed amendment is as follows:

1. Equality of rights under the law shall not be denied or abridged by the United States or by any State on account of sex.
2. The Congress shall have the power to enforce, by appropriate legislation, the provisions of this article.
3. This amendment shall take effect two years after the date of ratification.

The debate over the ERA, as was to be expected, centered more on the possible changes it might bring to women's roles and behavior than on equality of rights (Mansbridge 20). For example, Phyllis Schlafly, who became leader of STOP ERA, frightened many women with her assertion in the *Phyllis Schlafly Report* of November 1972 that "the Equal Rights Amendment will remove this sole obligation from the husband [to support his wife and children], and make the wife equally responsible to provide a home for her family, and to provide 50 percent of the financial support of her family" (quoted in Mansbridge 90). Though most ERA proponents considered Schlafly's interpretation absurd, they supported certain changes in family law. The ERA, as Jane Mansbridge points out in *Why We Lost the ERA*, would have invalidated existing legislation that defined the rights and responsibilities of a husband and father differently from those of a wife and mother (Mansbridge 91).

By the end of the 1970s, however, perhaps because of the public attention the ERA campaign brought to women's problems, those laws had been declared unconstitutional under the Fourteenth Amendment (Mansbridge 91). Women's roles and behavior were thus altered by the courts. Mansbridge argues that, although the ERA's defeat was "a major setback for equality between men and women" (Mansbridge 2), the campaign for its ratification raised consciousness among women and men, influenced state legislation, and ultimately effected a greater equality of opportunity for jobs and education than had existed before.

To change the structure that had afforded men opportunities it denied women to participate in civilization's intellectual discourse was to address the problem Woolf had described in *A Room of One's Own*. Repudiating the logic that men's contributions to poetry, painting, music, science, and philosophy indicated their intellectual superiority to women, Woolf ascribed the apparent differences in abilities to economic and legal relationships between the sexes. Other feminists have focused on long-standing social practices and deeply held prejudices that denied women access to the best research universities and libraries, that made publication more difficult for women than for men, that discouraged women from pursuing the education required for artistic or academic achievement, that channeled women into less intellectually challenging activities, that taught women to shun public attention, that instilled in women a sense of their own intellectual inferiority to men. These scholars are examining the "material things" that limit intellectual freedom.

Feminist linguists have persuaded academic and commercial publishing houses to avoid "sexist language"—such as the use of the male pronoun to indicate a person whose sex is unspecified, as in the sentence "Every citizen ought to exercise *his* right to vote." They have convincingly argued that traditional English usage implies a hierarchy of importance that functions in the minds of both men and women, perhaps at an unconscious level, to marginalize women. In the belief that sexual biases are maintained by our cultural discourse, academic feminists have joined political activists to change the discourse. The first step was to change the laws that have supported or permitted sexual discrimination.

♠ The Appreciation of Diversity

In the opposition to the Civil Rights Act and the Equal Rights Amendment we can detect the old concept of *types*, which Darwin's theory of natural selection had discredited in biology. The traditionalists assumed that the races and the sexes had essential features that defined their differences in absolute ways—that individuals were representatives of particular types. Because these types were permanent, uninfluenced by material conditions, the traditionalists believed that equality of opportunity would not affect the natural rank order of the races or the sexes. Neither could social change affect the individual's intellectual or moral capacity. They opposed the legislation for the social disruption it would cause.

In the arguments of the cultural holists, on the other hand, we can detect the evolutionary concept of *populations*. Darwin had substituted for the notion of immutable types that of categories of organisms, definable statistically rather than absolutely, and had shown that organisms adapted to changing environmental conditions; accordingly, there was no fixed, eternal order. For the cultural holists, existing racial and sexual relationships had evolved in response to the rules of society: To change the rules was to change the relationships and thereby the way that individuals conceived of themselves. They promoted civil rights legislation to modify the environmental conditions of human beings, with the expectation that individuals adapting to a new social structure, one less racist and sexist than the old, would differ in character from individuals suffering oppression or engaged in oppressing. To establish a social system in which citizens enjoyed the same rights and privileges and, ideally, had equal access to jobs and education was to make intellectual freedom possible for all.

The doctrine of species types had held in place not only a static conception of nature but also the notion of a divinely guided human universe. To some, for whom Darwin's dismissal of the typological concept meant "the death of God,"[4] the recognition of a cosmos where human evolution had occurred accidentally—and only recently—left no basis for morality. To others, however, that recognition transferred the responsibility for social justice from God to humans: In the absence of the faith in an unchanging, eternal order that had once allowed humans to assume an inability to rectify social injustices, humans have sole responsibility for the solution of society's problems.[5] This new responsibility offers hope for social justice in the future; after all, the moral system based on "the laws of God" had authorized for many people attitudes and behaviors that would now be described as perniciously racist. If there are not eternal types by which to evaluate individuals, then social prejudices have no natural foundation. Diversity is natural, even desirable. If there is not a natural "scale of ascent," the tendency to rank things is only a cultural habit. There is no natural law by which whites should be considered superior to blacks, or men superior to women; there is no natural law granting some humans the right to rule others.

Thus, in a universe of continuous flux, the structure of society may be changed, as those on the lower rungs of the social ladder have come to realize. Black liberation and women's liberation are only the most visible movements that have transformed social interaction in the past several decades. Spokespersons for gay/lesbian liberation have called attention to the way the heterosexual standard has socially marginalized homosexual individuals: In typological thinking homosexuality is considered a deviation from type. However, in population thinking, it is considered a variety of sexuality—and variety is natural. The effort to bring respect to the variety of individuals who make up human society, regardless of their sexual orientation, represents a holistic attitude founded upon population thinking.

We can also discern the shift to the population model in the campaigns of many other organizations to elicit appreciation for human diversity. To counteract the traditional, typological conception of "the American" as white, leaders of other ethnic groups in this country—such as the Chicanos and the

Native Americans, almost invisible in the public media until the 1960s—have worked to restore pride in their people's ancestry. They have done so not only through political action but also through publications and performances of their own poetry, song, and legend, exhibits of their cultural artifacts, and revisions of the standard accounts of America's past. Advocates for the physically disabled, who have successfully lobbied for legislation to make public facilities accessible to everyone, have shown us the many kinds of contributions that can be made by "differently abled" citizens whom we have formerly excluded from our work force.

While demanding a fully integrated society, one in which no one group is subordinated to another, the various "liberation" groups do not wish to eradicate human differences. They want a just social order, in which rights and opportunities are shared equally, without individuals having to conform to any particular type. They want the United States, in the metaphor of President Hannah Gray of the University of Chicago, to consider itself a salad bowl, not a melting pot. The melting-pot ideal was effectively typological, oppressive to those who did not dissolve and blend properly. In the population model, integration does not mean amalgamation; a healthy population is not characterized by sameness—whether of genes or of values, ideas, and cultural heritage. Instead, like any system, a healthy population is distinguished by productive interaction among its diverse constituents. And productive interaction is not achieved by the domination of one group over another.

Environmentalists are combatting the same model of domination that cultural holists are combatting, as Karen Warren shows in her explanation of *ecofeminism.*[6] Because the culture/nature dualism of the West has functioned to subordinate women to men by identifying women with nature, the rejection of that dualism brings about a new relationship not only of men with women but also of humans with nonhuman nature. In the holistic conceptualization of reality, the appreciation of diversity in nature entails a recognition of the interdependence of unlike beings. The various civil rights movements and the environmentalist movement are therefore philosophically compatible and mutually supportive.

The new model for social interaction brings both integration and respect for the uniqueness of the individual members. It is holistic in its understanding of society as a system whose components are interdependent. It is ecological in its acknowledgment of the value of diversity and the importance of cooperation: As ecologists know, a stable system, once its period of initial development is over, is marked more by a cooperation among its members than by the competition of individuals with each other. Cultural holists reject the dualism of spirit and matter, of mind and body, of intellectual capability and material circumstance, which produced the social hierarchies privileging men over women and whites over people of color. That dualism had predisposed us to see difference as absolute difference in value, or difference in rank on a scale, and to define relationships as oppositional. In assuming that the survival of a society depends upon the well-being of all of its citizens, cultural holists reject zero-sum thinking; and they evaluate a society's economic health on the basis of the well-being of all of its citizens, not on the basis of its stock market prices or its gross national product. Finally, cultural holists believe that social stability, or peace, requires social justice.

We must become global citizens.

—Carl Sagan, Oxford Global Survival

    Conference, 1988

3 ✿ Cultural Holism in the Academy

Not since the Russians launched their Sputnik in 1957 had the American system of education come under such criticism as it did in the 1980s. Thirty years ago, in an effort to compete with the Soviet Union militarily, the United States government dedicated massive federal funds to train youth in mathematics and science. In the 1980s, William Bennett, first as director of the National Endowment for the Humanities (NEH) and then as President Reagan's secretary of education, turned national attention, but without corresponding expenditure of money, to the humanities. Both efforts were motivated by nationalism: the desire to be the most powerful country in the world and the desire to have our citizenry appreciate its "cultural legacy." Now this nationalism has itself become the subject of debate.

At the end of the twentieth century, we are witnessing a fundamental transformation of our world order. The quest for military superiority has hurt the domestic well-being of the superpowers (actually bankrupting the USSR), and

Western chauvinism is being viewed by some as a hindrance to international cooperation. As Marshall McLuhan foresaw, the world is becoming a "global village." But in the transition conflicts develop between adherents to the old model for international relations and proponents of the new, between nationalists and "globalists." We have become familiar with that opposition in the antiwar demonstrations of both the Vietnam period and the present. The "patriots," who view the nation's health in terms of its competitive success, loathe the peace demonstrators for resisting the national resolve to "win"; and the peace demonstrators, who think of themselves as belonging to an international movement, loathe the flag wavers for glorifying military competition. The "victory" parades after the Persian Gulf war climaxed the surge of American nationalism but also elicited criticism from international organizations for appearing to celebrate the deaths of over a hundred thousand Iraqis.

The antagonism of nationalists to globalists is the basis of the recent controversies over the undergraduate curriculum. In the late 1980s, humanities faculty split into two angry camps, the traditionalists believing in the inherent superiority of the West in competition with the rest of the world, their opponents conceiving of human civilization holistically as a global community.

The Curriculum Debate

In *To Reclaim a Legacy*, a 1984 National Endowment for the Humanities report, Bennett argued that "the core of the American college curriculum—its heart and soul—should be the civilization of the West" (W. J. Bennett 30). As the West's major authors, Bennett listed Homer, Sophocles, Thucydides, Plato, Aristotle, Virgil, Dante, Chaucer, Machiavelli, Montaigne, Shakespeare, Hobbes, Milton, Locke, Swift, Rousseau, Austen, Wordsworth, Tocqueville, Dickens, Marx, George Eliot, Dostoevski, Tolstoi, Nietzsche, Mann, and T. S. Eliot. Of the literature and historical documents of the United States, he named the Declaration of Independence, the Federalist Papers, the Constitution, the Lincoln-Douglas debates, Lincoln's Gettysburg Address and Second Inaugural Address, Martin Luther King's "Letter from Birmingham Jail" and "I have a dream" speech, and works by "such authors as Hawthorne, Melville, Twain, and Faulkner" (W. J. Bennett 11). He concluded by adding the Bible.

Bennett was joined in 1987 by Allan Bloom, best-selling author of *The Closing of the American Mind*, in condemning the American educational system for young Americans' ignorance of Western masterpieces. In their opinion, the "leftists" who came of age during the 1960s had weakened the undergraduate curriculum by introducing, for political reasons, noncanonical texts into courses of Western literature and civilization: Feminists, ethnic minorities, and political radicals effectively deprived students of the traditional appreciation of our Western heritage that previous generations of students had obtained in college. According to Bennett and Bloom, in failing to transmit America's cultural "legacy," they had abandoned their responsibility to inculcate in students traditional American values. The time had come to bring order to American education.[1]

The problem, Bennett said, was that "intellectual authority [had been] replaced by intellectual relativism as a guiding principle of the curriculum" (W. J. Bennett 20). Bloom agreed, attacking feminists and leftists for "destroying the West's universal or intellectually imperialistic claims" (Bloom 39). Bennett and Bloom saw undergraduate education as "fragmented" and "chaotic" and advocated the establishment of a common curriculum to solve the problem. Bennett wrote:

> our eagerness to assert the virtues of pluralism should not allow us to sacrifice the principle that formerly lent substance and continuity to the curriculum, namely, that each college and university should recognize and accept its vital role as conveyor of the accumulated wisdom of our civilization. (W. J. Bennett 29–30)

Bloom wrote: "Of course, the only serious solution is the one that is almost universally rejected: the good old Great Books approach, in which a liberal education means reading certain generally recognized classic texts" (Bloom 344). Like their predecessor Arnold, Bennett and Bloom viewed "culture"—that is, Western "culture," which the humanities provided—as a mainstay against anarchy. Their remedy for the anarchy in the curriculum, and in society, was an authoritative reinstitution of the "the best that has been said, thought, written and otherwise expressed about the human experience" (W. J. Bennett 3).

Not unexpectedly, Bennett and Bloom drew fire from those they criticized. Feminists, ethnic minorities, political radicals, critical theorists, and even some mainstream humanities professors quickly challenged the neoconservatives' assertion that our cultural legacy was self-evident, consisting more or less of the great works Bennett had listed. They asked: Whose cultural legacy is it? In the United States one in four Americans now defines himself or herself as Hispanic or nonwhite.[2] Why should the literature curriculum omit slave narratives, the writings of the Hispanic settlers of this country, the writings of women? Furthermore, who decided what constituted "the best" written? What are the ideological values implicit in the traditional understanding of Western civilization? What is "the West"?

These questions came out of an ongoing critique of the literary canon, the critique Woolf had advanced with *A Room of One's Own*. The search for the answers involved an examination of the social context of the proclaimed "masterpieces" and, in the 1980s, an investigation into the ideological presuppositions of the various disciplines themselves. The so-called leftist scholars, most of whom I would call cultural holists for their holistic understanding of cultural discourse in a global community, had become increasingly aware that no discourse is free of ideology. According to their analysis, every writer thinks from within a particular social model of reality, writes from a particular position in society, and expresses particular interests and values. So when Bennett and Bloom accused them of having politicized the curriculum, the holists were well prepared to respond that the curriculum already embodied ideology. They were exposing that "canonized" ideology.

The cultural holists were actually redefining humanistic education. Their rejection of the traditional program for conveying "the accumulated wisdom of our civilization" represented not simply a disagreement over what constituted that wisdom or that civilization but rather a radically different notion of the purposes and methods of education. Whereas the traditionalists, who measured the success of American education by students' familiarity with a particular set of names and concepts, aimed to transmit an established body of knowledge (with traditional judgments of value), the holists, who could not measure success in any comparable way, aimed to stimulate habits of critical thinking about received opinion. Whereas the traditionalists promoted pride in our Western heritage, the holists promoted the appreciation of many cultures. To the traditionalists, the holists were relativists, engaged in discrediting Western values; to the holists, the traditionalists were absolutists, engaged in indoctrination.

This indoctrination consisted, cultural holists believed, of a "West-is-best" attitude rooted in the dualist model of political relations. The attitude inhered in the culture/nature dualism of Western imperialism, whereby Europe and North America conceived of themselves in an oppositional relationship to the lands they had colonized; in the individual/collective dualism that philosophically supported a hostile opposition to communist countries; and in the white/colored dualism that marginalized nonwhite, Hispanic, Native American, and Asian-American citizens of the United States. With the "we/they" habit of mind "we" dichotomized the world into people like "us" and people different from "us," and then in traditional humanities courses we studied and revered the former and gave little or no attention to the latter. Moreover, in his definition of "the civilization of the West" Bennett seemingly ignored the fact that the group comprising "us" Americans included Native Americans, African-Americans, Hispanic-Americans, and Asian-Americans.

According to the holists, to teach the older model was to perpetuate it in global politics, to the disadvantage of all. In the hope of a more peaceful world, higher education ought to instill in students a respect for other cultures rather than an uncritical assumption of Western superiority; and it ought to acquaint students with the ideas of people unlike themselves.

Since traditional courses of Western civilization and literature encouraged a Western chauvinism, cultural holists argued, those courses should be transformed into courses of world civilization and literature. Courses in American literature should be modified as well, to reflect the nation's ethnic and social diversity. Furthermore, instructors of literature should abandon the Arnoldian purpose of teaching only the "best" texts or, as Bloom put it, the "generally recognized classic texts," because that practice suppressed and implicitly denigrated the views of unrepresented groups. Only if we listened to the variety of the world's voices could we begin to understand the interests and values of those different from us.

The shift from the West-only orientation in humanities courses to the global orientation is an aspect of the culturewide shift from dualism to holism. At a Global Survival Conference, held in Oxford in April of 1988, Carl Sagan said, "We must become global citizens" (Vittachi 39). At the Oxford Town Hall spiritual leaders, including the Dalai Lama, Mother Teresa, and the archbishop of Canterbury, met with scientists, journalists, film makers, and educators from every continent of the earth to explore ways to save the planet. They learned from each other because they were all very different from each other, coming from different cultures and from different walks of life. They communicated well because, at least for the duration of the conference, they were globalists. The crisis they addressed, the survival of the human race, was too important for nationalistic competition; it demanded cooperation—cooperation and understanding.

This new model of social interaction, characterized more by cooperation than by competition, is gradually transfiguring higher education. The cultural holists, who are subversives to the many neoconservatives who favor strengthening the traditional curriculum, envision not simply new subject matter for courses but new teaching and research methods, new educational purposes, and expanded moral responsibility for the individual. In *The Closing of the American Mind*, Bloom noted: "Every educational system has a moral goal that it tries to attain and that informs its curriculum. It wants to produce a certain kind of human being" (Bloom 26). Precisely. The holistic educators wish to develop human beings better suited than previous generations have been to interact harmoniously with others in a global society.

ॐ   The Dualist Model

Deeply embedded in the two educational concepts, the traditional and the holistic, are thus two very different models of reality. Traditional education developed out of Western dualism.

Traditional teaching and research were founded upon the Western belief that one's intellectual life is independent of one's material circumstances, the belief Woolf challenged with her declaration that "intellectual freedom depends upon material things." The Cartesian separation of "self" from "world" provided for the confidence in objectivity that made possible empirical science. In the manner of naturalistic painting, the painting of fixed perspective, Cartesian dualism made "reality" appear "out there," clearly defined, replete with meaning, ready to be described and analyzed by the careful observer. The careful observer's material conditions—social status, race, gender, political relationship with the state—were therefore irrelevant to understanding the world. Truth was absolute.

According to this model, "knowledge" of the world could be accumulated atomistically and incorporated as "a body of knowledge." And although periodic scientific revolutions—such as the Darwinian revolution in biology or the Einsteinian revolution in physics—required reinterpretation of the accumulated data in a field of inquiry, scientists generally assumed that it was possible to discover the laws of nature, that it was possible to obtain truth: Consensus could be reached on the answer to a scientific question. Humanists too assumed that it was possible to know the truth of a sequence of events. For example, historians, working honestly and diligently with enough data, could theoretically narrate the whole of the world's past; the task was unachievable not because of the nature of writing history but because of the inaccessibility of complete information. For that reason, historians, like scientists, specialized in particular areas, with the expectation that collectively they could approach completeness. The word *history* was synonymous with the word *past*: A nation's "past" was its "history."

Essential to the dualist confidence in objectivity was the assumption that language could be used neutrally to convey information. Since Francis Bacon in the early seventeenth century had distinguished rhetorical from nonrhetorical language and had assigned the latter to science, most historians and scientists had taken for granted the transparency of nonrhetorical, or "ordinary," language. Ordinary language supposedly carried no values of its own, no ideology: It enabled a historian or a scientist to describe impartially a sequence of actions or a set of natural laws, and it reflected neither the ideology of its culture nor the particular viewpoint and values of the historian or scientist. It was this presupposition of linguistic neutrality that made knowledge itself appear value-free, without ideology, and that allowed historians and scientists to be convinced of their own disinterestedness. It made for certainty and a belief in absolute truth.

Ideally, professors ignored the political issues of the day to pursue truth in their fields of specialization. In fact, the principle of "academic freedom," imported from Germany in the late nineteenth century, was founded upon the dualist assumption that truth could and should be pursued in freedom from political pressure. Academic tenure insured professors the opportunity to speak the truth, whether or not the truth was popular, in the classroom; in return professors were to refrain from expressing "partisan" views.[3] The university was an "ivory tower" that protected the life of the mind from the material forces outside. Knowledge transcended politics.

Intellectual work in the dualist model, therefore, meant investigation of the world in a disinterested and apolitical manner. In the humanities, the purpose of scholarship was to interpret texts and events, and the purpose of teaching was to convey "the accumulated wisdom of our civilization." Despite the scholarly quarrels over "what really happened" here and there, or what this or that poem "really meant," the presupposition that the truth could be found made consensus theoretically possible. The accompanying presupposition that there was a right way to understand events and texts supported a vertical order of learning, for it justified an authoritarian transmission of knowledge from professor to student. It also provided for the educational goal of mastery of a field.

To see how the model has functioned in the undergraduate curriculum, let us imagine a traditional course in Western literature with a textbook anthology of works by the same great writers Bennett listed in *To Reclaim a Legacy*. The course's traditional instructors introduce the works as Western masterpieces, works that time has proven to be "the best"; and they teach them in a conscientiously apolitical fashion, focusing on their aesthetic qualities, the universal applicability of their themes, their philosophical arguments, their relation to each other, and perhaps the story they tell of "Western values." These literary specialists generally do not treat the literature as aspects of economic or political systems, because their responsibility is to focus on the writings themselves as literary "monuments" or as representatives of the West's aesthetic and intellectual tradition. In the dualist model, the aesthetic transcends the economic. (Marxist professors, of course, do not acknowledge that dualism, but they have always been a suspect minority.)

In treating the masterpieces in this way, the traditionalists adhere to the atomistic assumption that the works are intrinsically meaningful, intelligible independently of their social context. So, although they may vary the syllabus slightly—substituting Boccaccio for Chaucer, or Sartre for Mann, for example— the many professors teaching the course do not depart widely from each other in their interpretations of the works. They communicate more or less the same story, despite minor differences in their explanations of individual works, because the canon—that of the textbook anthology—holds in place a particular account of our culture's past, making other accounts seem "biased," politically motivated, patently wrong. Since, in this model, consensus has established the truth of the traditional understanding of Western culture, and since truth transcends ideology, anybody promulgating an unorthodox account appears to be expressing an ideological opinion. Professors are supposed to refrain from disclosing in the classroom any ideological opinions they may personally hold: The public expression of ideology is propaganda.

Most American colleges and universities have required for a liberal arts degree such a course as I have described, because in the traditional model knowledge of the Western intellectual tradition is considered synonymous with education. The underlying assumption is that unless the nation's educated citizens share a common body of knowledge, a common understanding of the history of our civilization, and a pride in our Western heritage, society will be fragmented into myriad groups unable to communicate with one another because of differences in interests and values. The neoconservatives, who continue to make this argument, believe that in order to have a unified culture, increasingly difficult to achieve in a multiethnic society, American schools and colleges should teach "certain generally recognized classic texts," texts that are paragons of intellectual discourse, conveyors of wisdom.

❧ The Holistic Model

Ecology offers a model for the new holistic study in the humanities. In the belief that systems cannot be understood through atomistic approaches, ecologists approach problems in teams composed of researchers with expertise in a variety of areas. A team whose members all possess the same information, the same attitudes, and the same perspectives is hardly more useful than a single individual. Furthermore, a team whose members share an assumption of Western superiority and an ignorance of other cultures will have difficulty working with teams from non-Western societies. Cultural holists, who like ecologists see the world nonatomistically, argue that the United States will be unable to understand either the world's structural problems or its own if its citizens all have the same vision of the world's past, the same bit of the world's "accumulated wisdom," and the same ideological posture. In the cooperative model, intellectual strength lies in intellectual diversity.

In the opinion of cultural holists, the attempt to achieve cultural unity by the imposition of a single version of history is not only foolish but actually dangerous; it is totalitarian. To demand that all literature professors, regardless of their views, teach more or less the same thing is to demand obedience to an intellectual autocracy. The authorization of a particular set of "masterpieces" as expressions of the culture's accumulated wisdom is an authorization of a particular story about the culture's past, a story representative of the viewpoint of the socially powerful. Scholars taking other texts to be the significant expressions of Western values will of course be proposing different stories, stories that may challenge conventional wisdom.

Authoritarian control of the academic intelligentsia is always difficult to accomplish, besides being ethically repugnant and contradictory to the principle of academic freedom. Yet most traditionalists would not describe a reinstatement of traditional humanities courses as intellectual despotism; instead, they would consider it a return to a unified educational program that once served, in their version of American history, a society relatively homogeneous in values. Such a return is impossible now without coercion. In the late twentieth century the multiethnic professoriat reflects an increasingly multiethnic American society, whose citizens inherit customs and values from cultures around the world. It includes not only white men, many of whom may plausibly consider the Western literary canon to be their "cultural legacy," but also many women and scholars of various colors and ethnic backgrounds who cannot. It includes political radicals who came of age during the Vietnam era and who learned to be suspicious of official opinion.

These scholar-teachers have begun to explore a wide range of texts that went unnoticed by those who measured the excellence of a work by its degree of resemblance to Western masterpieces. And they are generating new interpretations of texts and events, new histories, and new explanations for patriarchy, race relations, and American foreign policy. They are crossing disciplinary boundaries in teaching and research to connect literature with economic and political systems, scientific suppositions and discoveries, and military practices. They are developing a critique of Western dualism. To recover the old order, traditionalists would have to suppress the burgeoning of this nontraditional scholarship. They would have to use coercion.

The holists reject the notion that a uniformity of values, especially in a multiethnic society without uniformity of educational or economic opportunity, can be created by a uniform educational program. According to holistic thinkers, a vertical social order will never be characterized by uniformity of values because individuals develop values in relation to their particular circumstances. Just as "intellectual freedom depends upon material things," ideology develops in relation to social conditions. Since those suffering oppression of any kind do not share their oppressors' interests, they are unlikely to acquire their oppressors' habit of mind simply by reading the same books.

Nor will they do so by being forced to admire what their oppressors deem "the best." Holistic thinkers, to the dismay of their opponents, have abandoned the discipline's traditional purpose of studying only "the best" texts, and only "literature," for the following reasons. The designation of certain works as "literary" rendered them politically impotent in the classroom and subordinated all kinds of writing concerned with social circumstances. "The best" were selected by a generally privileged, ideologically homogeneous literary intelligentsia, who—like the nineteenth-century ethnologists—set standards by their own tastes, values, and interests. An ethnically and ideologically diverse professoriat, consisting of men and women, will not reach consensus on the best thought and written. Finally, the ranking of texts implies a hierarchical evaluation of cultures, races, and sexes that reinforces prejudices within the country and encourages Western chauvinism, whereas attention to all kinds of writings of people who are different from "us" leads to the appreciation of diversity.

Rejecting the dichotomy of the aesthetic and the political, holists examine the literary work in its social context as a product not so much of the individual author but of the author's culture. This orientation toward context has led to a practical obliteration of the dualist distinction between literature and nonliterature—and between high art and popular art—as well as a theoretical obliteration of the distinction between the literary work and its textual environment. As a result of the foregrounding of context, interest in authorial originality has yielded to interest in the text as the intersection of ideas, ideas of which the text's writer is never fully aware, since the writer's consciousness is also constructed by social forces. To express this shift in attention away from aesthetic object and toward social structure, many scholars have employed in their writing the word *text*, which may refer to a poem, a legal document, a history of a battle, or fragments of a woman's diary, for instance, instead of the word *work*, which traditionally referred to an individual's specific aesthetic creation.[4] With the concept of *intertextuality*, the flow of ideas through texts, cultural holists abandon the atomistic consideration of works in favor of analysis, through a variety of texts, of the discursive system. *Literature* gives way, as the object of study, to *culture*, and cultural understanding replaces literary knowledge as the discipline's primary purpose.

Behind this reorientation from the artwork itself to the discourse in which it is embedded is the theory that meaning is contextual. It is a relativist notion, that meaning is not intrinsic to things and events but rather humanly constructed; in fact, a nonatomistic understanding of phenomena can only be relativistic. The meaning of a text, for example, is unfixed; it depends upon the particular context (social, economic, ideological, philosophical, religious, etc.) in relation to which the reader reads it.[5] And the reader is himself or herself embedded in a particular context, within which he or she has developed expectations, interests, values—a model of reality. Since context is never fully definable, in part because it includes the observer, the meaning of anything is forever unstable. The universe has become "decentered," as Jacques Derrida has described the secular, post-Einsteinian world in which no absolute grounds meaning, a world in which—like words in a dictionary—everything obtains meaning in relation to everything else.

The acceptance of the relativity of meaning is the end of the dualist conception of order. The relinquishing of the belief in objectivity, which happened early in this century in the physics of Einstein and Heisenberg, has profound repercussions for both science and the humanities. If we must take into account the observer's position in any description of nature, we must take into account the observer's position—that is, values, interests, expectations, conceptual order, language—in any assertion of truth. As Benjamin Lee Whorf showed in his study of the Hopi Indian language, our very notions of time and space reside in our language.[6] Thus even language, in which we think and write about events, expresses ideology; to a degree that we cannot know, it structures our reality. What we discover about the world depends upon what we already believe, what we want to know, what we are technologically, philosophically, and linguistically prepared to understand, and what we are culturally pre-disposed to find. The Cartesian concept of an objectively definable reality that the observer can observe disinterestedly has become a myth: For the holist, "reality" is a cultural construct.

Humanistic knowledge, perhaps more obviously than scientific knowledge, reflects the particular material conditions—language, culture, class, race, and gender—of its makers. A course syllabus likewise reflects the particular values of the professor who designed it, and the texts on the syllabus reflect the values of their authors. Once we have recognized the relativity of what we formerly took to be truth, we cannot in good conscience present any set of texts as "the best." So, in the acknowledgment that texts reflect the socially derived values of their authors, cultural holists advocate exposing students to a variety of texts. In the absence of an absolute they decentralize the curriculum.

How would this work in a large university, for example, which offered nu-merous sections of an introductory world literature course in the period from 1700 through the present? Let us imagine such a course as taught by cultural holists. Each of the many instructors, whose ethnic, social, and educational backgrounds differ, develops a syllabus. One may include many of Bennett's favorites, perhaps with the addition of a few Latin American short stories, an African novel, and some Indian poetry. Another, focusing on East-West differ-ences, may include works by Voltaire, Dostoevski, Eliot, Sartre, and a number of Asian and Middle Eastern writers. A third, focusing on the development of feminism, may include texts by women and men from around the world that advocate a reconceptualization of the woman's function in society. A fourth, with the subject of Western imperialism, may juxtapose texts—texts that are well known and texts that are little known—from European, African, and Mid-dle Eastern writers to show political consequences of values. A fifth may explore poetry, novels, plays, manifestos, and documents of other sorts generated in periods of revolution.[7]

These instructors abandon, as an outmoded goal resting upon the possibility of objectivity, the traditional effort to "cover" a period of literature (such as Western literature from 1700 through the present). With the assumption that there is no objectivity, and therefore no single right way to understand or exemplify a period, the different instructors explore an age in different ways, taking different texts as their starting points, asking different questions of them. In the absence of a single right way to understand the world, the instructors take upon themselves and impart to their students the responsibility for making connections. In the holistic model the emphasis in teaching thus shifts from transmission of accumulated knowledge to stimulation of critical thinking, and the responsibility for learning shifts from teacher to student.

The students come to realize that their own questions generate new connections and therefore new understandings and that they learn by thinking critically. Having been made aware that there is no absolute truth, they gain respect for interpretations of texts and events advanced by others, including persons very different from themselves. Without the dualist belief that a given body of knowledge transcends politics, they become sensitive to ideology by criticizing texts representative of multiple viewpoints. In juxtaposing previously unconnected texts, not all of which may have been classified as "literature," students come to think of texts not as autonomous units of fixed meaning, or as apolitical artworks, but as socially enmeshed expressions of cultural values, expressions of particular constructions of reality. Because they have not all studied the same material and acquired the same attitudes and methods, they may bring to future discussions of problems a variety of perspectives, providing for teams of thinkers the diversity that is required to analyze systems.

With today's information technology the intellectual diversification of society is inevitable, as is the end of Cartesian dualism. Instant copying allows instructors to assemble from the world's writings their own classroom "textbooks" to support unconventional analyses of culture and to stimulate the criticism of received views. Whereas commercially produced and widely adopted textbooks, by establishing a uniformity of course content, had reinforced the assumption of an objectively definable reality, the new technologies, which provide access to any text extant in the world and thereby facilitate infinitely variable course content, undermine that dualism; they undermine confidence in single explanations for events. Just as the printing press transformed European consciousness in the sixteenth and seventeenth centuries by reifying the culture's knowledge, separating the knower from the known, computers and copiers, now at least as accessible to the public as books were then, are accelerating the present revolution in Western consciousness by distributing through society opportunities for the construction of knowledge and the publication of opinion.[8] Thus technology, as much as the changing racial character of society, will defeat the traditionalists' program for a Western-masterpiece curriculum.

The holistic model of learning is a model for social action. Whereas the dualist dichotomy of knowledge and politics had given traditional education the appearance of being above politics, the holistic connection of knowledge and politics makes education subversive, disruptive of social practices based on unquestioned assumptions. In fact, any pedagogy calling for students to look to social context is ultimately subversive. Whereas the purpose of humanistic education in the dualist model was to interpret texts and events, its purpose in the holistic model is to change the world. Neoconservatives are right to call the cultural holists political radicals, for whether or not the latter engage in overt political activity, in calling attention to ideology in texts and in encouraging critical thinking in students they undermine the vertical social order. They are antiauthoritarian.

Just as heightened nationalism is a reaction to the globalization of society, the neoconservative drive to reinstate the teaching of the nation's "cultural legacy" is a reaction to cultural holism. Yet the vehemence of the attack on the holists suggests that more is at stake than the humanities syllabus. The recent crusade against multiculturalism, like the campaign against liberalism in the 1980s, reveals a hostility toward efforts to consider society as an interactive whole, a hostility on the part of individualists who equate shared responsibility for the community with socialism. The cultural holists' attention to the West's conceptual order is finally what most frightens neoconservatives. By viewing discourse as a seamless web, they address the whole whenever they examine any part: To obtain an understanding of the big picture is their ultimate objective. The success cultural holists have had in elucidating the relationships of cultural values to social circumstances—in connecting Western aesthetics with social inequities, for instance—indeed threatens those with investments in the vertical order.

Neoconservatives have good reason to fear cultural holism, because the perpetuation of the nation's present distribution of wealth and power depends on atomistic approaches to its problems. It depends, for example, on a refusal to see racism, poverty, illiteracy, and environmental pollution as effects of a particular conceptual system. The demand that literature professors confine their interests to the canon reflects, therefore, not only a desire to preserve the country's traditional cultural identity but also a desire to suppress analysis of the social order. Holism, with its aim of understanding the interdependence of all of a system's components, exposes the injustice of an order of dominance.

Education for Global Citizenship

The traditional concept of humanistic education is typological. In typological thinking an unchanging ideal, such as the species type, transcends the world of diversity and change; organisms that depart from their type in appearance or behavior are considered deviant. In his call to teach "the best that has been said, thought, written and otherwise expressed about the human experience," Bennett set up the Western masterpieces as atemporal—and therefore apolitical—ideals, worthy of study for their superiority to all other writing. The masterpieces expressed truth. Texts that departed from the ideals in form or ideology were deviant: Traditionalists might criticize some of them as uninteresting, others as poorly written, unsophisticated aesthetically, propagandistic, or expressive of nonuniversal experiences. In dualist terms, these presumably inferior texts belonged not to the realm of society's intellectual life but to the material realm of its political life.

The vertical order prescribed the purpose of the humanities requirement in undergraduate education: the individual's acquaintance with the best thought and written. By acquiring a knowledge of the great books and a sophistication of aesthetic taste—in short, by becoming "civilized"—individuals assured themselves of higher rungs on the social ladder than those who remained uneducated, "primitive." In a competitive society, where individuals strove against each other for wealth, power, privilege, and prestige, individuals sought education for their own benefit. Since "time" had already selected "the best," the humanities curriculum offered more or less the same "knowledge" to every individual obtaining a liberal arts education. That knowledge marked the educated type. Accordingly, it was logical for Bennett and Bloom to interpret a modification of the traditional curriculum as a weakening of it.

The conception of life as a competition, at the root of Western imperialism, supported not only the orientation of humanistic education toward the individual but also the orientation of the program toward the West. During the many centuries when travel between Europe and non-Western lands was difficult, Western civilization constituted the subject matter for university education because Western civilization (which in the Middle Ages included aspects of Middle Eastern culture) was basically all that European scholars knew. In the twentieth century, however, when we have access to all parts of the world, the continuation of the West-only humanities curriculum represents a redefinition, a radical narrowing, of our intellectual objective: from seeking knowledge of the vast and fascinating world to knowing and admiring our own culture. This redefinition evolved naturally, in part because of our inheriting the curriculum of our predecessors, in part because the larger world, which technology has made increasingly accessible, is too vast for any single individual to know, but also in part because of the competitive habit of mind. The West-only curriculum now serves to reinforce a patriotic appreciation of Western civilization, beneficial only if we see ourselves in competition with other civilizations.

Instead of educating for patriotism, holists educate for the appreciation of cultural diversity. Not simply a practical response to the impossibility of agreement on a core content for humanities courses, this alternative is a strategy to achieve peace within a multicultural society and in a multicultural world. Obviously, it is fundamentally antiauthoritarian. A multiculturalist definition of American society, one that accounts for the multiple cultures that form it, does not provide ideological support for the currently dominant group's political power, at home or abroad. To neoconservatives who identify those in authority with the state and fear that a decline in the authority of the traditionally powerful group within the country will translate into American weakness in international competition, globalism threatens the nation's unity and hence its security.

For cultural holists, however, a nation's strength—its unity—comes from the efficient functioning of its various components: that is, the harmonious interaction of all its citizens. The assumption that the nation can be unified only if the many ethnic groups that make up its population adopt the same "American" values has denigrated all those Americans for whom the ideas and customs we have labeled "American" and have found in the "best" literature seem foreign. In such an environment ethnic groups must either abandon the ideas, customs, language, and artistic expression unique to their culture in submission to the dominant culture or labor aggressively to preserve their identity in a nation that officially does not respect it. And the assumption that harmonious relationships among different cultures of the world depend upon uniformity of values or of economic system has led the United States into relationships of either dominance over or antagonism toward those nations wishing to have a different political system. Neither relationship encourages respect for the different culture; neither supports the health of the whole. At the end of the twentieth century, with the renewed struggles of ethnic groups everywhere to preserve their cultural autonomy, any attempt on the part of one culture to suppress others is, for the holists, both immoral and fruitless.

Holists reject the assumption that peace requires uniformity. That strategy for peace and harmony came out of a vertical order, held in place by domination, whereby those at the top determined appropriate thought and behavior and tried to impose their values on those beneath them on the ladder. Peace, then defined as absence of overt conflict, depended upon the acquiescence by the powerless to the powerful. In the newer model, individuals are educated to appreciate differences and to expect from others a divergence of views and behavior. Ideally, education for global citizenship will foster the establishment of nonoppositional relationships both within the nation's multicultural society and among the varied peoples of the world.

The Western faith in objectivity has led us to assume that there was a right way to see things and that we Westerners were discovering the truth. We therefore interpreted ideas about the world that differed from our own, particularly if they came out of cultures different from our own, as quaint or politically motivated or wrong. This absolutism made getting along with cultures whose national goals were at odds with ours exceedingly difficult, for it disinclined us to hear what they were saying. As a holistic world order replaces the vertical order, in which the militarily powerful spoke mainly to each other, a more inclusive conversation will develop, one in which everybody gets to speak. The opposite of an absolutist confidence in our own moral and intellectual authority is a willingness to participate nondomineeringly in international discussion.

Respect for others unlike ourselves is an aspect of *relativism*, inappropriately maligned by absolutists as an abandonment of moral responsibility.[9] I understand relativism, however, to mean a holistic (nonatomistic) conception of reality in which the definition of anything is relative to its context: It is a conception of interconnectedness. An understanding of the world as continuously changing, inhabited by diverse populations who conceive of it in diverse ways and who are economically, politically, and ethically tied to each other in a global system, entails social responsibility: If we see the world as a system, we cannot dismiss the problems of any group as unrelated to our own behavior. Relativism is implicit in cultural holism.

I would like to inform all the intrepid Muslims in the world that the author of the book entitled The Satanic Verses, *which has been compiled, printed and published in opposition to Islam, the Prophet and the Koran, as well as those publishers who were aware of its contents, have been sentenced to death.*

I call on all zealous Muslims to execute them quickly, wherever they find them, so that no one will dare to insult the Islamic sanctions. Whoever is killed on this path will be regarded as a martyr, God willing.

—*Ayatollah Khomeini, February 14, 1989*

4 &. Literature in a Global Society

The global society has accelerated the emergence of holistic thinking in the West, replacing the model of individual autonomy for international relationships with one of interdependence. Easy travel and widespread migration contribute to an intermingling of races and cultures in all the industrialized countries and in many of the developing nations; and instant communication connects all parts of the planet. More than ever before, cooperation among the planet's diverse inhabitants is necessary if the human race is to survive through the next few centuries. Yet, at the same time that intellectuals cooperate in pursuing knowledge and in seeking solutions to global environmental problems, powerful political, economic, and religious forces perpetuate international, intercultural, interregional, and interracial competition. The very efforts holistic thinkers make to promote cooperation and mutual respect among cultures are being interpreted by some of those cultures as attempts to destroy their traditional identities.

The furor over Salman Rushdie's novel *The Satanic Verses* starkly reveals certain perils attending the transition from a world of cultures separated by linguistic, religious, racial, and geographical barriers to a world of cultural interpenetration. In this new world, individuals of all faiths and cultures live everywhere, establishing communities in countries whose beliefs and values are foreign to their own and attempting, despite great difficulties, to maintain their identities. Paradoxically, global communication, while permitting a more and more holistic understanding of events by the international intelligentsia, magnifies and exacerbates ideological disagreements among the diverse cultures, within nations and between nations, because it enables the words of any individual to reach a world audience. Like it or not, a writer speaks to the world. Rushdie spoke to the world with his book, and so did the Ayatollah Khomeini with his *fatwa*.

The fundamentalist Muslims' response to *The Satanic Verses* represents, in the extreme, a resistance to the globalization of society. Rushdie describes it as a resistance by "apostles of purity" to the forces of "mongrelisation" (Rushdie, "In Good Faith" 53). The belief in a single right way to see the world, to behave, and to worship impels fundamentalists to seek ideological purity, to resist amalgamation and integration with those of other persuasions in the same way that white racists seeking racial purity restrict their contact with other races. Fundamentalists whose sacred scripture teaches that theirs is the only true religion will naturally view other beliefs as dangerous and will define religious tolerance as the absence of faith. From the purists' perspective, the holists' professed respect for the belief systems of various cultures indicates a contempt for what they themselves hold sacred.

The Ayatollah's edict has generally been treated by Western writers, for whom censorship is anathema, as an abridgment of free speech rather than as a response that a culture struggling to preserve its identity made to worldwide social change. When analyzed as a conflict between the desire for "purity" and the forces of "mongrelisation," however, the event epitomizes the clash between traditionalism and cultural holism. The "apostles of purity" are protectors of their own traditions, and the representatives of "mongrelisation" are advocates of cultural interaction, which threatens the integrity of any single culture.

The Rushdie incident thus reveals the global implications of American curriculum battles.

Rushdie, born to a Muslim family in India and educated after the age of fourteen in England, was already a prizewinning author when he published the 547-page novel *The Satanic Verses* on September 26, 1988. *The Satanic Verses* was itself a finalist for the prestigious Booker Prize (which Rushdie's earlier novel *Midnight's Children* had won) when Syed Shahabuddin, a member of the Indian Parliament, described it as an "indecent vilification of the Holy Prophet" (Appignanesi and Maitland 33) and persuaded Prime Minister Rajiv Gandhi on October 5 to ban it. India was followed by Pakistan, South Africa, Malaysia, Egypt, Saudi Arabia, and other countries of the Middle East. In January of 1989, protesters in England held a public burning and demanded that Viking-Penguin, Rushdie's publisher, withdraw and pulp all outstanding copies of the book. On February 13, police killed five Muslims in a violent anti-Rushdie protest at the U.S. Information Center in Islamabad, Pakistan.

On February 14, Iran's Ayatollah Khomeini issued his *fatwa*, or edict, calling for Rushdie's death. An Islamic charity organization promptly offered a reward of one million pounds to any non-Iranian, and three times as much to an Iranian, who carried out Khomeini's order.

What was in *The Satanic Verses* that so offended the Islamic community? The title of Rushdie's novel refers to a legendary message given to the Prophet Muhammad by the Devil, who had posed as the Archangel Gibreel; according to Islamic tradition, when Muhammad learned of the deception, he revoked the "satanic" verses and substituted for them the "true" verses that now appear in the Koran. In *The Satanic Verses*, one of Rushdie's two protagonists, Gibreel Farishta (Gabriel Angel), a psychotic Bombay film star who has become a superstar in the film genre of "theologicals," dreams that he, as the archangel, speaks to Mahound on Mount Cone. Mahound (that is, Muhammad, whom Gibreel calls by the derogatory nickname medieval Christians used who considered him a heathen idol) is a businessman from Jahilia, a city of sand, "the quintessence of unsettlement, shifting, treachery, lack-of-form" (Rushdie, *Verses* 94). In his fantasy the actor Gibreel plays both parts, that of the angel and that of the Prophet, inseparable in Gibreel's mind at the moment the message is uttered. But Gibreel the dreamer knows that he, Gibreel, is not "God's postman": "God knows whose postman I've been" (Rushdie, *Verses* 112). Mahound returns to Jahilia, where drunken revelry marks the last day of the festival of Ibrahim, enters the poetry tent, and with eyes shut recites some verses.

The next day Mahound again climbs Mount Cone, where out of his passionate desire to get the truth he engages Gibreel in a wrestling match. Both of them are naked. "[A]nd let me tell you," says Gibreel, "he's getting in *everywhere*, his tongue in my ear his fist around my balls, there was never a person with such a rage in him, he has to has to know he has to KNOW and I have nothing to tell him" (Rushdie, *Verses* 122). Gibreel finally pins the Prophet to the ground: "and then," says Gibreel, "he did his old trick, forcing my mouth open and making the voice, the Voice, pour out of me once again, made it pour all over him, like sick" (Rushdie, *Verses* 123). After awakening from his "customary, exhausted, post-revelatory sleep," Mahound says aloud to the empty air that it was the Devil, Shaitan, who had come to him the first time, who had tricked him by appearing in the guise of the archangel, who had given him not godly but satanic verses. Mahound knows that this time, however, the angel was real, because the angel wrestled him to the ground. Mahound hurries back to the city to strike the satanic verses from the record. And he founds the religion known as Islam, or "Submission."

Later in Rushdie's novel Gibreel again dreams that he appears to the Prophet, in order to give rules for Mahound to pass on to the faithful: rules about what to eat, how to sleep, which sexual positions to use, how to slaughter animals, how to bury the dead, how to divide a dead man's property. In the fantasy, one of the Prophet's scribes, Salman, who doubts whether the rules actually come from Allah, decides to test Mahound. When Mahound dictates a verse in which God is "*all-hearing, all-knowing,*" Salman writes "*all-knowing, all-wise*" (Rushdie, *Verses* 367). After Mahound has finished, Salman reads the chapter back to him. Disappointed that Mahound has not noticed the alteration, Salman realizes that he is writing the Book himself, polluting God's word with his own profane language. Salman continues to make changes, on one occasion even substituting *Jew* for *Christian*, until finally the day comes when he sees puzzlement in the Prophet's face, and he realizes that he has gone too far. Rather than destroy himself in exposing the Prophet, he leaves town and saves both.

Although the Mahound chapters constitute only part of an extremely complex novel, difficult for even the reader accustomed to postmodern literary experiments, they are of course the ones that have captured the attention of the Islamic community. In these chapters Rushdie mocks the Islamic belief that the Koran contains the exact words of Allah; in suggesting that the rules of Islam originated in faulty transcription of the Prophet's revelations, Rushdie ridicules the theological foundation for Muslim culture. By portraying Muhammad's moment of divine inspiration as the climax of a homoerotic wrestling match, when the angel's voice spills onto Mahound's body, Rushdie associates Islam with sexual submission. (The word *Islam* in Arabic means "submission" or "surrender" to God; *Muslim* means "one who surrenders.")

Islamic publications excerpted passages from the novel to show that Rushdie had also pictured Muhammad with a whore, that he had called Muhammad's companions "bum" and "scum," that he had given the names of Muhammad's wives to prostitutes in a brothel, that he had had the archangel approve "sodomy and the missionary position," that he had given the name of Jahilia to Mecca. (In Islamic discourse *jahiliya* refers to the age of ignorance that preceded the establishment of Islam, but for modern fundamentalists it also means the contemporary Muslim world, whose people they find arrogant and impious. For modern doubters, on the other hand, *jahili* means the combination of ignorance and religious certainty; Ruthven 41.)[1]

Reports of Rushdie's fictional depiction of Muhammad stirred Islamic fundamentalists into a frenzy. They accused Rushdie of "false" interpretations of the Koran and "wrong" portrayals of Muhammad, of an insincere exploration of "reality," of "incompetent" characterization of the Prophet and of the Prophet's companions, of filthy language, of blasphemy, of satanism, of deliberate distortion of the "truth," and, again and again, of "arrogance" (see reviews collected in Appignanesi and Maitland). Shahabuddin declared that *The Satanic Verses* "serves to define what has gone wrong with the Western civilisation—it has lost all sense of distinction between the sacred and the profane" (Appignanesi and Maitland 38).

On February 15, the day after the Ayatollah sentenced Rushdie to death, Iran's Hashemi Rafsanjani explained the book as part of a First World, Zionist-inspired conspiracy to destroy Islam; he said that Zionist publishers had paid Rushdie in advance, had appointed bodyguards for him, and had garnered for the book the publicity necessary to make it sell well, with the aim of breaking "the sanctity of Islam and all that is sacred in Islam."[2]

On February 16, Rushdie issued the following statement:

> As author of *The Satanic Verses* I recognise that Moslems in many parts of the world are genuinely distressed by the publication of my novel. I profoundly regret the distress that publication has occasioned to the sincere followers of Islam. Living as we do in a world of many faiths this experience has served to remind us that we must all be conscious of the sensibilities of others. (Appignanesi and Maitland 97–98)[3]

Khomeini did not accept the apology. On February 19, he proclaimed: "Even if Salman Rushdie repents and becomes the most pious man of time, it is incumbent on every Muslim to employ everything he has got, his life and his wealth, to send him to hell" (Appignanesi and Maitland 99).[4]

Rushdie was guilty of blasphemy in the eyes of religious Muslims, even in the eyes of those who disputed the Ayatollah's sentence.[5] However, many Muslims who described themselves as "secular" were also outraged by the book, because Rushdie had treated the Islamic tradition with disrespect in front of a world audience. Instead of reinforcing Islamic identity, as some Muslims have argued that Islamic writers ought to do, Rushdie questioned it. In fact, he celebrated— in his own words—"hybridity, impurity, intermingling" (Rushdie, "In Good Faith" 53). By satirizing the supposedly sacred account of Islam's religious origins, Rushdie had asserted that there was no divine sanction for the culture and therefore no "purity": The culture's identity rested upon a myth.

In an essay he contributed to *Newsweek* in February of 1990, Rushdie told why he had felt compelled to satirize religious orthodoxy:[6]

> Throughout human history, the apostles of purity, those who have claimed to possess a total explanation, have wrought havoc among mere mixed-up human beings. Like many millions of people, I am a bastard child of history. Perhaps we all are, black and brown and white, leaking into one another, as a character of mine once said, *like flavours when you cook.* (Rushdie, "In Good Faith" 53)

The exposure of the historical basis for a culture's claim to "purity" is necessary to disarm its apostles.

❧ The International Debate

It would seem that Rushdie, an atheist and self-described "mongrel," is technically not a blasphemer. Only if *The Satanic Verses* is considered an "offense against the faithful"[7] can it qualify as blasphemy. But it is with this interpretation of blasphemy that a number of Christian and Jewish religious leaders united in their opposition to the novel, some of them calling for a ban; the disrespect Rushdie had shown the Muslims they took to be disrespect toward the faithful of any denomination.[8] While condemning the Ayatollah's method of censorship, they endorsed his motive, which was to protect the integrity of his religion.

Yet numerous Muslims who were likewise offended by Rushdie's novel took Rushdie's side. They felt that Khomeini's edict was doing more to turn world opinion against the Islamic peoples than Rushdie's novel could possibly do, for it reinforced the stereotype of Oriental ruthlessness. Naguib Mahfouz, the Egyptian winner of the Nobel Prize for Literature in 1988 who was himself regarded as an apostate by religious zealots, described Khomeini as a terrorist who exploited the ignorance and illiteracy of the masses. He joined a number of Islamic intellectuals, both in the East and in the West, in condemning the fatwa as illegal. Government officials of Egypt, Turkey, Iraq, and Kuwait objected to the edict, some of them denying Khomeini's authority to represent the Muslim population. A Palestinian leader said that the death threat encouraged individuals to align themselves with Rushdie.

In New York, while several European publishers were delaying publication of the novel in translation and some booksellers were refusing to sell it, thousands of writers signed their names to a statement supporting "the right of all people to express their ideas and beliefs and to discuss them with their critics on the basis of mutual tolerance, free from censorship, intimidation and violence" (Appignanesi and Maitland 110). On February 22, 1989, Article 19 (a London-based international organization dedicated to monitoring censorship), the Authors Guild, and American PEN sponsored a public reading of *The Satanic Verses* and criticized President Bush for failing "to condemn forthrightly and unequivocally the attempt to murder Salman Rushdie and his publishers" (Appignanesi and Maitland 152). At this meeting, Gay Talese led the 500 people inside the New York loft and the 3,000 people gathered outside, who were listening to the proceedings via loudspeaker, in the Lord's Prayer (Decter 20). In early March, after the bookstore chains Barnes & Noble, B. Dalton, and Waldenbooks had removed copies of the novel from their shelves, the United States Senate passed Resolution 72, committing itself to "protect the right of any person to write, publish, sell, buy and read books without fear of intimidation and violence," calling the fatwa "state-sponsored terrorism," and supporting "the publishers and booksellers who have courageously printed, distributed, sold and displayed *The Satanic Verses.*"

To Islamic fundamentalists the freedom of expression the international literary community espoused meant freedom to insult their religion, their way of life; it was as offensive to them as their fundamentalism was to the promoters of tolerance. What the West saw as an act of individual artistic expression they saw as an act of war, initiated on behalf of the Western powers by an apostate Muslim living in the West. The apparent willingness on the part of Rushdie's supporters to hear all the world's voices and to facilitate publication, translation, and worldwide distribution of all kinds of writings signified a skepticism of any dogma. Moreover, Talese's recitation of the Lord's Prayer constituted an implicit declaration that the Judeo-Christian religious tradition was superior to the Islamic.

The Muslim testament of faith, that "there is no God except Allah, and Muhammad is the apostle of God," is not in accord with an appreciation of other constructions of reality. No absolutism is. It was a conflict, the Indian scholar Homi Bhabha said, "between the cultural imperatives of Western liberalism and the fundamentalist interpretations of Islam, both of which seem to claim an abstract and universal authority" (Appignanesi and Maitland 112).

However, to view the conflict only in terms of the opposition of fundamentalism to liberalism is to simplify a complex problem intrinsic to cultural holism: the competition between the principle of free expression and the principle of respect for those with different views. These principles are not mutually supportive. To uphold the principle of free speech, a society must allow the expression of disrespect; to prohibit the latter is to abandon the former.

At the February 22 meeting of PEN and the Authors Guild, the Palestinian Edward Said, a professor of English at Columbia University, recognized the irreconcilability of the two principles when he asked rhetorically a question that has been posed again and again by Muslims:

Why must a Moslem, who could be defending and sympathetically interpreting us, now represent us so roughly, so expertly and so disrespectfully to an audience already primed to excoriate our traditions, reality, history, religion, language, and origin? Why, in other words, must a member of our culture join the legions of Orientalists in Orientalizing Islam so radically and unfairly? (Appignanesi and Maitland 166)

For centuries Muslims had had to defend themselves against the West's scorn of Islamic culture—and its ignorance of it—and Rushdie had exacerbated that unfortunate relationship. Nevertheless, Said declared, it was imperative that Rushdie's safety and his right to write about Islam as he saw fit be insured: Democratic freedoms should not to be abrogated to protect Islam (Appignanesi and Maitland 166).

Disagreement among Muslim intellectuals over the competing demands has recently appeared in the pages of scholarly journals. In an essay published in the *Yale Journal of Criticism* Agha Shahid Ali, a poet teaching at Hamilton College who describes himself as a secular Muslim, argued that Rushdie had betrayed Islam. In his opinion, "Condemning fundamentalism is a noble enterprise; provoking it is not." He wrote that it would have been more "useful" for

Rushdie, instead of insulting the Islamic people, "to bring Muhammad into the twentieth century to expose the abuses of a Khomeini." "Rushdie has missed a great opportunity," he said, "particularly on behalf of secular Muslims who are tired to death of Khomeiniites and their shadows on the one hand and the Western portrayal of Muslims on the other" (Ali 296).

In the same issue Akeel Bilgrami, a philosophy professor at Columbia, responded that for critics to impose such a restriction upon an Islamic writer would itself be "Orientalist."[9] Furthermore, for Muslims to refrain from criticizing the governing assumptions of Islam—or of any other culture—would be patronizing. Comparing Rushdie with the antireligious film makers Arrabal and Buñuel, who used their art "to undermine the seemingly perpetual conserving tendencies of bourgeois European culture," which rested on Christian beliefs, Bilgrami argued that Rushdie's project of criticizing orthodoxy necessitated offense to the Islamic devout.

The quarrel over Rushdie's book illustrates the potential for hostility that accompanies the transgression of traditional boundaries for individual expression. But it illustrates as well the inevitability of such transgression in a world where writers physically or intellectually exiled from their homelands feel compelled to describe the worlds they know. Since a culture's identity resides in the histories its own people have told of its past, when its writers offer new ways to think about the past the culture's identity will be threatened. Those faithful to the old histories will naturally interpret the critique as disloyalty, betrayal, blasphemy, or untruth—in sum, disrespect.

❧   Literature in a Global Society

Westerners have inherited from the dualist model the conviction that objectivity is possible and that the truth is knowable, separable from partisan opinion, or ideology. At home and abroad, Americans have defended free speech as a means—the best available—to obtain truth. With the need to distinguish empirically truthful statements from other socially meaningful utterances, we have traditionally compartmentalized "speech" into science, history, journalism, propaganda, religion, literature, and myth; and our understanding of any utterance or text is governed by our awareness of the category to which it belongs. We appreciate fiction when it is labeled *fiction*, writing that is designed to be empirically "untruthful"; we do not when it is labeled *science, history,* or *journalism.* Thus the category forms an essential part of a text's context, determining its standing in our discourse. Our promotion of free speech as a universal goal rests in part on a naive assumption that other cultures employ generally the same theoretical distinctions within their discourse.

The distinction between aesthetics and politics, which postmodernists are now challenging, is peculiarly Western. One of its consequences is the relative impotence of literature in the American classroom. Even though such works as Harriet Beecher Stowe's *Uncle Tom's Cabin*, Kate Chopin's *The Awakening*, and Richard Wright's *Native Son* have served political purposes, alerting the public to human suffering that might be alleviated by changes in laws and attitudes, Americans consider the novel to be primarily entertainment. The Cartesian belief in the possibility of objectivity obligated traditional authors to declare their intentions, to distinguish stories of their imagination from accounts of "reality." So novelists adopted the custom of prefixing their fiction with a disclaimer like the following:

> This is a work of fiction. The characters, incidents, and dialogues are products of the author's imagination and are not to be construed as real. Any resemblance to actual events or persons, living or dead, is purely coincidental.

With such a paragraph (which, incidently, Rushdie did not include in *The Satanic Verses*), authors obtain their readers' consent to "lie." And, of course, the better the authors "lie"—within the category of fiction—the more we applaud their imagination.

We traditionally take the author to be an *individual* whose work will naturally appeal to some readers and not to others, because different writers have different ideas, literary skills, interests, and values, and different readers have different tastes. In the text designated as fiction the author may create characters whose opinions and actions offend readers, may present unpopular views of cherished religious and social beliefs, and may try, through plot, imagery, or rhetoric, to convince us to relinquish our own conventional attitudes about the world. Except in the case of pornography, which generates intense disagreement, we have assumed that the author has the right to do so in a "free society." Most of us simply abandon the books we dislike to save time for the books we like. Even when we find ourselves the object of a satire, we Westerners usually dismiss the offensive material as fiction, the opinion of an individual, nothing worth fighting over. After all, "art" is not "real."

The international outcry over *The Satanic Verses* demonstrates that this concept of art is specifically European-American. Art is "real" to those cultures that have not separated art from politics and have not privileged it as the product of an individual's unique imagination. Literature is politically powerful in oral societies and in societies lacking a legislated freedom of the press, and it can be dangerous to totalitarian regimes. Where there is oppression, art can be the voice of the oppressed; where there is belief, it can stimulate questioning—and disrespect.

The Iranian reception of *The Satanic Verses* substantiates the axioms of contemporary critical theory that meaning is contextual and that the interpreter is part of the text's context. In the context of Western aesthetics, *The Satanic Verses* was interpreted as an artwork, and it was defended as such. In the context of world politics, the novel was interpreted as a political attack on Islam, and its author and publisher were sentenced to death on those grounds. Rushdie had no control over the interpretation his heterogeneous world audience would give his book, nor could he even insist on an appropriate context for his readers to interpret it. Once his book entered societies with other ways of organizing discourse it was bound to be interpreted politically.

Of course, Rushdie wrote *The Satanic Verses* for political reasons. The Muslims were not incorrect in seeing the novel as a political attack on Islam, for Rushdie had intended, by way of "literature," to move his audience to a critical examination of Islamic culture's foundations. In effect, by treating as myth what his fellow Muslims had long considered historical truth, he was attempting to undermine the religion's social power. Thus, at the same time that he was defending himself against the hostile fundamentalists by arguing that *The Satanic Verses* was fiction, to be read as such according to Western aesthetic conventions, Rushdie was asserting—in earnest—that the Muslims' most basic beliefs were also fiction.[10]

The striking differences in the societies participating in the global conversation, all of them sending and receiving texts, make obvious to both Western and non-Western thinkers the provinciality of Western aesthetics. When we see the ideological content of other societies' art, and the uses to which it is put, we are forced to acknowledge that our own art is ideologically laden as well, although its ideology may be more difficult for us to perceive. Contemporary critical theorists, no longer governed by spirit/matter dualism, have argued that no discourse is free of ideology, simply because every utterance issues from a particular, culturally rooted position. The global expansion of the audience for art bears this theory out.

Much of the fundamentalist Muslims' initial criticism of Rushdie's book revealed their lack of acquaintance with Western literary conventions. Those who said that Rushdie did not rely on "scientific and logical arguments," that he did not use "objective methods of research," and that he distorted "historical facts" (quoted in Pipes 110–111) were, in fact, relatively unfamiliar with the novel as a literary form and with the practice of interpreting fictive events in the context of the fiction. They did not put *The Satanic Verses* into the category of literature. Rushdie's defense of his literary depiction of Muhammad—that it was embedded in the dream of a fictional character losing his mind—made no sense to them. They took the excerpted passages to represent the author's opinion and took the author to represent the West. They saw no reason, after learning of the blasphemy, to read the whole of *The Satanic Verses* since they already knew it to be untruthful, and dangerous. They did not distinguish between literature and political statement, between literature and history, or between literature and blasphemy. Nor did they distinguish between the supposed blasphemy and an assault on their civilization, because they do not differentiate between their religion and their state.

Americans have difficulty understanding the impact on Muslims of Rushdie's portrayal of Muhammad. We officially—and conceptually—separate church from state, and we recognize a diversity of religions within our multicultural society. Although some Americans want laws to prohibit flag burning, our courts have historically upheld the First Amendment's guarantee of freedom of expression. Our universities, through the principle of academic freedom, safeguard the free exchange of ideas in order to promote originality of thought. Except in a few instances, such as the McCarthy witch-hunt for communists, we have given the individual's right to free expression priority over cultural homogeneity. After all, our country was founded by religious dissidents.

The combination of our individualism, our aesthetics, our categorization of discourse, and our system of government may have rendered us in the West immune to the kind of shock *The Satanic Verses* produced in Islamic fundamentalists. But we cannot ignore their reaction to the book simply by dismissing them as absolutist or literarily naive; nor can we say that their reaction was peculiarly Muslim. That would be to continue an imperialist imposition of Western values on other cultures and thus to perpetuate the Western "arrogance" that angry Muslims detected in Rushdie's novel. After all, in the United States, demonstrations over Martin Scorsese's film *The Last Temptation of Christ* moved Blockbuster Video not to stock it. What we must try to see is the relationship between the profound desire of conservatives in various cultures, including our own, to maintain the coherence of their traditions and the threat posed to those traditions by worldwide cultural integration.

The Ideology of Cultural Holism

In a global society the dynamic opposition, which has long structured the internal politics of nations, between the drive for purity and the willing acceptance of heterogeneity becomes globally consequential. Now, with the varieties of humankind "leaking into one another . . . *like flavours when you cook,*" the process of cultural and racial change quickens. And the resistance to such change grows intense.

Within the United States academic holists have had to contend with the Western traditionalists' nostalgia for purity, implicit in their ethnically exclusive—in effect, typological—definition of Western culture, their presumption of Western superiority, and their conviction that education should reinforce Western identity. Holists view this Western chauvinism not only as an invitation to conflict with other cultures but also as a racist denial of the cultural contributions to the West from non-Westerners. It is not accidental that the proposal to achieve cultural unity by returning to a traditional education in Western "masterpieces" comes at a time when our country's population of ethnic minorities is increasing. The desire to preserve purity—a purity that never was—comes out of a fear of integration and change. And it signals a longing for stasis and cultural definition that is unattainable in any population, particularly in an age of widespread migrations.

In the discipline of literary study the traditionalists' stand against the holists' acknowledgment of cultural instability parallels the nineteenth-century anti-evolutionists' opposition to the theory of evolution. The antievolutionists held that an unchanging ideal order stabilized nature, and the evolutionists saw nature as flux. Twentieth-century traditionalists strive to preserve the West's traditional identity (which they take to be white European and North American), whereas the holists accede to continuous change. Nineteenth-century theologians said that the evolutionists were atheists; twentieth-century literary traditionalists say that the holists, who teach all kinds of writing, fail to revere literature.

Indeed, the holists, in their effort to hear all the world's voices, not just the West's and not just those of the West's "masterpieces," treat no text as sacrosanct. They believe that no text stands outside political, social, economic, and philosophical systems, which are all in continual metamorphosis. Cultural holism represents the philosophical egalitarianism Shahabuddin attacked with his accusation that Western civilization had "lost all sense of distinction between the sacred and the profane." Actually, Shahabuddin was conflating the ideology of Rushdie and the Western holists with the ideology of the Western traditionalists. Western traditionalists fail to understand the effect upon Muslims of *The Satanic Verses* not because they consider nothing sacred but because they categorize the book as literature, not theology. The holists are the ones who do not partition reality into the sacred and the profane, who ignore generic boundaries, and who express the "secularism" fundamentalist believers in both the East and the West detest. They are relativists engaged in exposing the historical basis for any claim of "purity."

However, the term *secular* is problematical: It arises out of the dualist model in which *secular* opposes *spiritual* and *profane* opposes *sacred*. Cultural holists treat such revered texts as the Bible and the Koran as neither sacred nor profane. Like contemporary geneticists who see organisms as unique members of evolving populations, they see the Bible and the Koran as unique representations of particular belief systems in an evolving global system of texts. In the context of Islam, the Koran is a sacred text, a document whose function within that society is unique; in the context of world politics, it may be compared with texts held sacred by other peoples. It is the respectful attention to the world's system of texts, combined with an appreciation of cultural diversity, that is inconsistent with acceptance of any religious orthodoxy and incompatible with nationalism.

Secularism—or rather, relativism—is thus prerequisite to a genuine appreciation of cultures other than one's own. Because the spirit/matter dualism had functioned to exclude non-Western writings from the canon, for not expressing "universal values," it is only by abandoning that dualism that Western holists can bring non-Western writings into the curriculum. It is only by disregarding the West's tacit rank order of human expression, held in place by Western dualism, that holists can bring Islamic poetry, for example, into the literature classroom of American universities. Paradoxically, in showing respect for the expressions of all cultures holists risk being considered disrespectful toward what any one culture, including their own, holds sacred.

Cultural holists may want to teach *The Satanic Verses* for the book's insight into the dilemma of the Muslim apostate living outside the Middle East, for its satire of religion, or for its postmodernist playfulness. But most Muslims, with a justification women and minorities can understand, fear classroom instruction in literature that mocks their beliefs and customs, because such instruction can institutionalize prejudices. Furthermore, Rushdie's celebration in his novel of "hybridity, impurity, intermingling," which is in keeping with the holists' appreciation of genetic and cultural heterogeneity, strikes at the efforts of Islamic traditionalists to build esteem for Islamic values. Rushdie's satirical depiction of the origins of Islam, which holists concerned with the origins of myths may enjoy, is likely to offend believers of all faiths.

What is becoming obvious in the American humanities curriculum controversy is that because all texts embody ideology any text may offend one group or another. *The Satanic Verses* mocks Islam, but so does *The Divine Comedy*, a Western "masterpiece" that pictures Muhammad in hell. Voltaire's *Candide* is anti-Semitic, and so is Shakespeare's *Merchant of Venice*. From the feminist viewpoint much of the Bible is sexist; so is the philosophy of Aristotle. *Huckleberry Finn* has been called racist by left-wing critics and has been removed from some high school libraries, and *The Wizard of Oz* has been banned by right-wing critics for its "secular humanism." Clearly, the diverse value systems of twentieth-century readers differ from those of the authors of these works. Neither authors nor readers transcend the politics of their times. Holists, who recognize the inescapability of ideology, therefore acknowledge the potential offensiveness of any book. However, with the assumption that ideological homogeneity is not desirable, or even possible without oppression, holists opt for offense over censorship, since in their model censorship amounts to suppression of variety—by whichever advocates of "purity" have the power and authority to force their own beliefs upon others.

In short, cultural holists, by promoting cultural exchange on a global scale, pit themselves against traditionalists around the world who wish to maintain their own long-standing social orders. For this reason, cultural holism is subject to attack from all sides: from representatives of non-Western societies, who view it as a new version of Western imperialism, and from defenders of traditional "American" values, who view it as a leftist assault on the academy.

Cultural holists have a political agenda; it is to diminish global animosities through intercultural understanding and respect. Since the uncritical teaching of any text may instill in students the values embodied in that text (thus perpetuating racism, for instance), academic holists advocate situating the text in its political context. To their traditionalist opponents who say that they "politicize" the masterpiece, they respond that the "masterpiece" already embodies ideology. To teach a "masterpiece" as politically embedded is not only to deprive it of its aura of abstract authority—and thereby to undermine the reverence that students might otherwise have for it—but also to sensitize students to ideology and to make them critical. Simultaneously, this approach restores to texts some of the social import the texts had when they were written and enables students to obtain a critical distance from them. Ultimately, the practice allows teachers to introduce all kinds of texts from the world's diverse and evolving populations as illustrations of the variety of deeply held views. It enables the professor to teach *Huckleberry Finn* without encouraging racism and *The Satanic Verses* without vilifying Islam.

❧ Intermingling

Opposition to traditional higher education has taken a variety of forms, some of them more separatist than holistic in their orientation. Yet ethnic separatism, which traditionalists fear will lead to cultural fragmentation and hence to national disunity, is also a sign of the changing model for social interaction in the United States.

Black colleges are now attracting increasing numbers of students eager to learn about the culture of their ancestors. The undergraduates of many universities with large minority enrollments (such as the University of California at Berkeley, whose diverse racial minorities compose 55 percent of the student body) are splintered into separate ethnic organizations, which encourage their members to associate mainly with each other. Oberlin has established separate dormitories for African-American, Hispanic, and Jewish students. At Vassar, in June of 1991, black students held their own graduation ceremony (De Palma). Centers for African-American studies, Chicano studies, Native American studies, and the like are proliferating, and their faculties are motivated not only by a desire to investigate their cultures' heretofore disregarded contributions to American civilization but also by a desire to build cultural pride.

This ethnic separatism[11] does not represent a rejection of the United States' efforts to become an integrated society. It does represent, however, a resistance to the country's present model for integration in which ethnic minorities are expected to adopt the customs and values of the majority. Ethnic separatists want to intermingle but not to blend. We should not be surprised that groups that the dominant culture has previously isolated and denigrated are now exploring strategies to win the respect that members of the dominant culture have always enjoyed.

From the viewpoint of the globalist, ethnic separatists have something in common with right-wing traditionalists, here and elsewhere; they are all striving to preserve their cultures' identities in a rapidly changing environment. However, because the social order the American traditionalists wish to retain has historically entailed the subordination of minority ethnic groups to the majority, the aims of the ethnic separatists and the traditionalists are mutually incompatible. Whereas the American traditionalists struggle to uphold a hierarchical order, which has served well upper- and middle-class whites, the ethnic separatists are pushing for a new, more egalitarian social order in which the uniqueness of their particular cultures may be appreciated.

Dissension is intrinsic to change. Any transformation of a culture's model of reality will involve social upheaval, and the conversion of a culturally partitioned planet to a global society will involve global discord. The free exchange of ideas, like the exchange of genes among populations, naturally causes changes in the cultures, changes that traditionalists resist and that holists accept as natural. Holists see cultural stasis as unnatural. Their hope is that eventually a widespread appreciation of diversity and a preference for cooperation will supplant the intercultural competition that now predominates.

In the holistic model everything must be considered in terms of its function in dynamic systems. For cultural holists, as for post-Darwinian biologists, there is no transcendent ideal order governing either nature or culture: Human communities evolve in relation to each other just as do the constituents of ecosystems. There is no intrinsic hierarchy of cultures any more than there is a scale of ascent in nature. There are no culturally static populations of humans any more than there are permanent genetically homogeneous populations of organisms of any kind; there are no ideal cultural types; there is no purity. Intermingling—of genes, and of ideas, values, languages, religions, and models of reality—occurs in time.

But such intermingling does not lead to global sameness. It leads, as it has always led, to new varieties. The anticipation of a worldwide cultural homogeneity is as dangerous as the hope to regain an imagined lost racial and cultural purity, since both expectations can be used to justify oppression. And the attempt to preserve a particular cultural or genetic order in a world of continuous change leads inevitably to conflict. Cultural diversity is as natural as biodiversity and similarly must be recognized as valuable to the functioning of the whole.

Holists assume that we are *all* genetically and culturally "mixed-up human beings"; we are all hybrids, impure and intermingled. The challenge is to intermingle peacefully.

None of the funds authorized to be appropriated pursuant to this Act may be used to promote, disseminate, or produce—

(1) Obscene or indecent materials, including but not limited to depictions of sadomasochism, homoeroticism, the exploitation of children, or individuals engaged in sex acts; or (2) material which denigrates the objects or beliefs of the adherents of a particular religion or non-religion; or, (3) material which denigrates, debases or reviles a person, group, or class of citizens on the basis of race, creed, sex, handicap, age, or national origin.

—Helms amendment

5 ❧ The Backlash

A new way of thinking tends to provoke a defense of the old. Just as the Victorians saw in Darwin's theory a threat to their concept of order, so traditionalists see in cultural holism a threat to their entire system of values—to conventional notions of social hierarchy, of racial relationships, of masculinity and femininity, of authority. The socioeconomic advances made by women and members of minority groups through equal opportunity legislation, the changes in the workplace and the family brought about by increased educational opportunities for the previously marginalized, the gay/lesbian liberation movement, the international peace movement, the international environmentalist movement, and the fundamental critique of the society's accumulated wisdom—all of these aspects of cultural holism have generated a broadly based vocal and occasionally violent resistance.

When a culture's long-standing model of reality is in upheaval, radical antagonism will develop between those fighting hardest to save the old order and those fighting hardest to bring about the new. The opposition between nationalism and cultural holism is manifesting itself now in the controversy over "multiculturalism," in colleges and universities and in institutions channeling federal money into the arts and humanities. On the right, critics of multiculturalism have derided their ideological opponents as "politically correct persons," lumping together both the extremist and the more moderate promoters of diversity. They have waged a broad attack on higher education in general—on the content of humanities courses, the quality of teaching, the research mission of the university, and the "liberal bias" of the faculty.[1] On the left, scholars continue to teach and write about the racial and sexual attitudes implicit in Western discourse, taking as a major intellectual responsibility the criticism of the political status quo. In an attempt to combat what they determine to be an increase in racist, sexist, and antihomosexual verbal assaults on campus, some academic administrators have instituted antiharassment codes to enforce a respect for differences.

The exposure of ideology in intellectual discourse, which the right condemns as "the politicization" of learning, is itself an aspect of a holistic construction of reality. Traditionalists calling for a return to a supposedly apolitical search for truth are in effect expressing a nostalgia for the dualist model, which distinguished between the realms of ideas and politics; in that model neither art nor the humanities was thought to be able seriously to affect the culture's political and economic life. Now the right, however, as well as the left, is connecting knowledge and politics.

Seeing the cultural holists' social critique as a threat to social stability, neoconservatives have initiated a major campaign to control the expression of antiauthoritarian ideas. The campaign's unstated purpose is to preserve the hierarchical social order.

ᚖ Mapplethorpe and the NEA

The debate in Congress in 1989 and 1990 over the reauthorization of the National Endowment for the Arts exemplifies the conflict between the old order and the new. At the center of the controversy was a retrospective of the work of Robert Mapplethorpe, whose travel and exhibition costs the NEA had partially subsidized. Aggressively questioning accepted attitudes toward racial relationships, sexual behavior, the clean and the dirty, and art and pornography, Mapplethorpe's photography constituted an offensive challenge to the values of traditionalists. Senator Jesse Helms, who claimed to speak for the many Americans who were (or would have been) repelled by the pictures, crusaded to end public support of "obscene and indecent" art. The besieged NEA, numerous arts organizations, and various professional societies in the humanities opposed him on the grounds of protecting artistic freedom.

In the hostility to Mapplethorpe's art and to multiculturalism can be discerned the same fears of relativism and cultural flux that marked the opposition to Darwinian evolution and later to the various civil rights movements, the fears that now mark the resistance to global cultural change. It is the same play, but with different players: The defenders of the old order understand the world in terms of types; the proponents of the new understand it in terms of continuous cultural and genetic evolution. The former resist change, because change threatens established cultural values and customs; it threatens their identity. The latter accept change as natural and inevitable.

Using as examples of NEA-funded art Andrés Serrano's *Piss Christ* and Mapplethorpe's homoerotic photographs, Helms proposed in July of 1989 "the Helms amendment" to the fiscal 1990 appropriations bill for the Interior Department and related agencies; the Senate approved it on July 26. By October, however, after various organizations in the arts community had lobbied against the amendment, Congress passed a compromise bill that retained only provision (1) of Helms's original paragraph, minus the words "or indecent," which were eliminated during the debate. It prohibited the NEA from funding in the 1990 fiscal year "materials which in the judgment of the NEA may be considered obscene, including but not limited to depictions of sadomasochism, homoeroticism, the sexual exploitation of children, or individuals engaged in sex acts and which, when taken as a whole, do not have serious literary, artistic, political, or scientific value" (Tessier 311).[2]

A year later Congress abandoned the content restrictions when it reauthorized for three years both the National Endowment for the Arts and the National Endowment for the Humanities. The government nonetheless retained some control over federally subsidized art by requiring that grant recipients return to the NEA any money used in the creation of a work that a court subsequently ruled "obscene."[3] The NEA panels awarding the grants were to take into consideration "general standards of decency and respect for the diverse beliefs and values of the American public." Although most arts supporters regarded the new rules as an improvement over the Helms stricture, some said that freedom of expression had already been curtailed, because in the present climate of political conservatism the NEA would be increasingly reluctant to fund provocative art (see Myers A19).[4]

Why has this controversy erupted now? Art history textbooks record the erotic depiction of nudity in Western "masterpieces," in Japanese woodcuts, in the sculpture of so-called primitive societies which exaggerate the size of male and female sex organs. Pablo Picasso's erotic etchings are famous. Marcel Duchamp's entry of a urinal titled *Fountain* in a 1917 exhibition is appreciated as a significant philosophical statement about the social construction of art.[5] Audiences have often expressed displeasure with art that violates their "general standards of decency," but their reactions have been chronicled as testimony to the power of the artwork—in the art world. Seldom has an artwork scandalized the "real world."

Although Helms cast the debate as one over the expenditure of public funds, he represents to the art world the neoconservative campaign to control the transformation of American society, the same campaign William Bennett initiated in the mid-1980s to reinforce "American values" in the humanities curriculum. Certainly, in a time when government dollars were needed to address the country's widespread poverty, illiteracy, and environmental pollution, Congress's budgetary decisions deserved intense scrutiny. However, the fact that many backers of the Helms amendment appeared more eager to prohibit desecration of the flag than to spend the money necessary to begin to alleviate those problems indicated that other issues were involved. What became obvious during the national discussion was that the Mapplethorpe exhibit had become the site for a clash between two opposing social models: a hierarchical order that would ideally outlaw the unconventional portrayal of sex organs and individuals engaged in homoerotic behavior and a philosophically more egalitarian order in which an artist would be free to attack traditional prejudices. It was also a clash between a conception of nature in which homosexuality is abnormal, and therefore to be controlled, and a conception of nature in which homosexuality is a variety of sexuality.

The retrospective of Mapplethorpe's photography called "Robert Mapplethorpe: The Perfect Moment" sparked the furor over NEA sponsorship of homoerotic art. Organized by the Institute of Contemporary Art in Philadelphia, the show had received a $30,000 grant from the NEA to help cover travel and display costs, a grant which came to the nation's attention when the Corcoran Gallery in Washington broke an agreement to host the show. The exhibition had been scheduled to open there on July 1, 1989, but on June 13 the Corcoran's director, Christina Orr-Cahall, canceled it, in fear that the publicity Mapplethorpe would generate, at a time when the far right was already questioning the authority of the NEA, might jeopardize the museum's NEA funding. On May 18, Senator Alfonse D'Amato had denounced the NEA on the

Senate floor for its grant to Serrano, and on June 9, Pat Robertson had asked his Christian Broadcasting Network viewers to urge Congress to end NEA support until it could insure that the endowment would never again fund "patently blasphemous" art. Ironically, by trying to avoid the attention the Mapplethorpe retrospective would bring to the museum, Orr-Cahall precipitated a demonstration against the Corcoran by members of the arts community, who accused her of bowing to political pressure. Meanwhile, another gallery, the Washington Project for the Arts, obtained the show for three weeks, from July 21 through August 13, during which time some 40,000 people saw the photographs. Thus Mapplethorpe's art was accessible to the senators who voted on July 26 for Helms's amendment (Phelan 4–7).

Mapplethorpe's work had received much critical attention from the art world during the 1980s, well before Helms introduced it to the general public. Between the early seventies and the late eighties (that is, until his death in March of 1989), Mapplethorpe had become famous for his stylized photographs of carefully posed flowers, faces, and nude bodies, both white and black. When Janet Kardon, then director of the Institute of Contemporary Art, asked him in an interview about his choice of subject matter, he claimed that his intention, whether shooting flowers or penises, was to obtain a beautiful composition: "When I've exhibited pictures, particularly at Robert Miller Gallery, I've tried to juxtapose a flower, then a picture of a cock, then a portrait, so that you could see they were the same" (Kardon 23).[6]

The Mapplethorpe retrospective included photographs of celebrities, of flowers, of white and black naked men and women, of naked children, and of men engaged in sadomasochistic acts. It contained a series of photographs titled *Manfred, 1974*, in the third of which the naked Manfred exhibits his erection; a photograph titled *Larry and Bobby Kissing, 1979* of two clothed white men kissing, and another titled *Embrace, 1982* of a black man and a white man, naked from the waist up, hugging; a photograph titled *Ken and Tyler, 1985* showing from the left side the naked bodies, but not the heads, of a white man and a black man in identical dance positions, one behind the other, as if in a ballet; several photographs of Lisa Lyon, who had previously won the "First Women's Body-Building Championship," and of the bodies of other naked or partially dressed women; a set of four photos titled *Ajito, 1981*, which depict, from front, back, left, and right, a naked black man sitting on a pedestal in a pose reminiscent of Rodin's *The Thinker*; a photograph titled *Thomas and Dovanna, 1986*, which pictures a naked black man waltzing with a white woman, whose hand holds the full skirt of her formal gown; several self-portraits, one from 1980 that features Mapplethorpe in women's makeup with bare shoulders, another from 1983 in which the artist wears a black leather jacket and carries a machine gun, and the last from 1988 in which, in an apparent reference to his impending death from AIDS, his head appears suspended in the darkness a few inches from his right hand, which holds the carved-skull handle of a cane. *Jesse McBride, 1976* is a picture of a young boy, six or seven years old, sitting naked on the back of a chair; the photo is of the sort one might find in a family album. The exhibition's most famous image, and perhaps its only humorous one, was *Man in a Polyester Suit, 1980*, which shows the dressed torso of a black man whose penis protrudes from his fly.

In 1988, New York's Whitney Museum of American Art had sponsored a Mapplethorpe exhibition that, in the opinion of some, was even more provocative than the Washington show. It contained the now famous photograph titled *Brian Ridley and Lyle Heeter, 1979*, which depicts two men in black leather, one holding a whip over his enchained partner; the photograph titled *Jim and Tom, Sausalito, 1977–78*, which portrays one man urinating into another man's mouth; and the *Self Portrait, 1978* of Mapplethorpe with a bullwhip stuck into his anus.

Mapplethorpe was a highly sought-after photographer, widely acclaimed for his portraits: of Laurie Anderson, Willem de Kooning, Louise Nevelson, Paloma Picasso, Donald Sutherland, Andy Warhol, and other celebrities. His flower studies were called "exquisite" (Sischy 77). But it was of course his "pornographic" work that drew the most commentary. For example:

> Though Mapplethorpe can subversively (and successfully) imply that a cock can as well be the subject of a portrait as a face, his isolation of limbs and areas of the body, and his frequent obscuring of the face in shadow or by means of the pose, does point to a deep nexus in his work where the tendency to see people as objects is both an aestheticizing into sculpture and an eradication of personality which is a characteristic of pornography.—Alan Hollinghurst, *Robert Mapplethorpe: 1970–1983*, 1983 (Hollinghurst 12)

> As things turned out, pornography was to be for Mapplethorpe what soup cans were to Andy Warhol: a guaranteed fast track to media recognition. Mapplethorpe's graphic documentations of New York's sado-masochistic gay scene marked the first time that such images had been recorded with such formal precision and artistic flair. . . .
> In the end, Mapplethorpe's sexual photographs, despite their novelty,

seem capable of commenting more on what is fashionable than anything else. His photographs are not comments on pornography or homosexuality or gender or even sex, but merely a rather flatly rendered and unimaginative diary of a life preoccupied with "getting turned on."—C. S. Manegold, *Arts Magazine*, Feb. 1984 (Manegold 96, 98)

However renegade some of Mapplethorpe's subjects have been, the fact is that he has accumulated a broad and deep sense of visual history, of the images and objects that are both "in" and "out" of the temples of taste.—Ingrid Sischy, *Robert Mapplethorpe*, 1988 (Sischy 78)

Mapplethorpe is an idealizer, a photographer of classical impulse and detachment who is fascinated with the poetry of proportion and the music of the body. He brings to almost all his pictures exquisitely balanced rhythms of light and shadow and beautifully calculated arrangements of shape.—Mark Stevens, *New Republic*, Sept. 1988 (Stevens 27)

What is interesting is less the phallocentrism of Mapplethorpe's aesthetic than the politicizing of that aesthetic, preeminently in the images from the late 1970s. . . . That was a period in which gays were coming out of the closet in large numbers, defiantly and even proudly, and were actively campaigning not only to change social attitudes toward themselves but to build their own culture. It seems clear to me that these photographs were political acts, and that they would not have been made as art were it not the intention to enlist art in some more critical transformation.—Arthur Danto, *Nation*, Sept. 26, 1988 (Danto 248)

A certain smart elegance—intense but never forced, aggressive, on the verge of being cloying but rarely falling over into sentiment or pretense—has always been the hallmark of Robert Mapplethorpe's work.—Charles Hagen, *Artforum*, Nov. 1988 (Hagen 140)

As Arthur Danto noted, Mapplethorpe's art, for all the praise it has won for its "elegance," appears politically motivated. By its unusual imagery, it calls into question not only our society's notions of tasteful subject matter for artistic representation but also its notions of appropriate behavior. Mapplethorpe is testing his audience's appreciation of aesthetic form when he chooses as the content of his art the parts of the human body our society wishes to keep hidden. In making the *display* of his subject's sex organs the subject matter of his photographs, he differentiates himself from traditional painters of nudes, and in doing studio portraits of males in homoerotic or sadomasochistic poses, he commemorates practices that are unacceptable to the general community. As reviewers have pointed out, Mapplethorpe is not surreptitiously taking snapshots of individuals unaware of being photographed; he is collaborating with his subjects in the creation of art. His camera not only records his cooperative subjects' presence in front of the lens but also attests to his own presence behind it. Obviously, Mapplethorpe aimed to shock.

The fact that until 1989 his work shocked relatively few, even in the art world, reveals certain dualist habits of thought that characterize American culture. Traditionally distinguishing art from "the real world," Americans have considered art an enhancement of the quality of life rather than an integral component of social discourse. Since the beginnings of modernism in the late nineteenth century, when painters abandoned realism in their preoccupation with form, ordinary citizens have tended to find contemporary artistic experimentation unintelligible and therefore unrelated to their concerns. They can easily disregard art about art. The art they do enjoy, such as the representational art of the great masters or the art of famous modernists like Picasso, has lost whatever power it may once have had to shock.

Within the art world Mapplethorpe was regarded as one more of the twentieth century's many iconoclasts. Some critics could concentrate on describing Mapplethorpe's technical brilliance, because they were accustomed to evaluating artworks for their formal qualities. Others, taking seriously his political intentions, could write about his subject matter thoughtfully and unemotionally, because they were accustomed to the time-honored artist's goal of *épater le bourgeois*—to shock the ordinary citizen. However they wrote, reviewers of Mapplethorpe's shows could assume that the great majority of citizens would remain ignorant about his accomplishments. Until 1989 Mapplethorpe's political statement was seen primarily by those already educated to art. Unlike Rushdie, who had the fortune (or misfortune) to live to see his novel reach the community whose values he was attacking, Mapplethorpe died before the media brought his message to the American people.

Mapplethorpe's message was a fundamental assault on the mode of thinking that for Helms constituted "decency." Moreover, it was an assault on Western dualism, which in its distinction between spirit and matter has relegated to the category of the "dirty" the parts of the body devoted to procreation and excretion. In Mapplethorpe's vision, a flower, a penis, and a face are "all the same," all parts of nature. Mapplethorpe rejects the Western tradition of portraying the

Negro as exotic, or "primitive" (as in the *National Geographic* photographs of naked Africans), a tradition which has its roots in the culture/nature, intellect/instinct, white/colored dichotomies; he presents the blacks, as he does the celebrities and the flowers, as studio models.[7] He suggests black and white coupling in *Thomas and Dovanna*, which mocks the racist fear of the black man's rape of the white virgin. He challenges conventional expectations of femininity in his photographs of the muscular Lisa Lyon, and he repudiates America's ostracism of homosexuals in his photographs of men embracing.[8] In short, Mapplethorpe opposes with his art the "apostles of purity," who retain typological concepts of gender, race, and sexuality. Like Rushdie, he represents the forces of "mongrelisation," which threaten traditional values.

Because Mapplethorpe celebrates a way of thinking about human behavior that is offensive to the majority, his photography constitutes a political act. And because realistic photography is much more accessible to the uninformed public than painting or literature, Mapplethorpe's work has awakened the public to the fact that art embodies ideology, that particular artworks may be dangerous because they may influence individuals' opinions and actions. In the dualist model the conceptual separation of art from politics to some extent protected artists and art lovers from an unsympathetic public, a public which in the United States was generally more occupied with business than with the art of the day. In turn the separation protected that public from contemporary art. The "real world" and the art world could coexist peacefully, as could the "real world" and the "ivory tower." But as artists abandoned modernist abstraction and as academics developed their sweeping critique of Western ideology, the increasingly conservative public, alerted earlier by William Bennett to the changing content of the college curriculum, was easily aroused against the NEA.

Public Institutions and the Holistic Model

No one should have been surprised that Mapplethorpe's defiantly antiauthoritarian art might provoke those in authority to attempt to suppress it. It was indeed "indecent," probably to most of the NEA's supporters as well as to Helms's; it was meant to be "indecent." But Helms said that his intention was not to suppress, or censor, "indecent" art, simply to stop the government's support of it.

There is a fundamental difference between government censorship—the preemption of publication or production—and governmental refusal to pay for such publication and production. Artists have a right, it is said, to express their feelings as they wish . . . but no artist has a preemptive claim on the tax dollars of the American people; time for them, as President Reagan used to say, "to go out and test the magic of the marketplace." (From Helms's address to the Senate, July 26, 1989, excerpted in Tessier 313)

Congress was persuaded.

Helms's rationale could be baldly stated as a principle of business: One should not pay for what one does not want. The taxpayers should not pay for art they do not wish to see. Yet, even presented in this way, without reference to the specific targets of the Helms amendment (depictions of sadomasochism, homoeroticism, and so forth), the argument begs certain questions: Who decides what the taxpayers wish to view and to pay for? Who decides what constitutes the art to which the public should have access?

These questions have led Helms's critics to cry "censorship." On March 21, 1990, Wayne Lawson, executive director of the Ohio Arts Council, testified before the House Education and Labor Subcommittee on Postsecondary Education that the Helms amendment would "stifle the arts":

If the Arts Endowment finds itself forced to restrain from entertaining applications to support the broadest possible artistic expression, and artists restrain themselves from proposing work that is risky or provocative, public support for the arts would become no more than a source of dollars available only to the most broadly acceptable.

The only federal grantees would be an establishment of official artists and official arts organizations. What is truly American in our system of support for the arts would thereby be destroyed with a resulting centralized governmental ministry of culture replacing our essentially democratic citizen-driven system. . . . Only safe art will be funded, and stimulating, challenging work will be left out. (Excerpted in Tessier 313)

For Lawson, Helms's attempt to regulate the content of federally subsidized art amounted to government censorship, because it denied provocative artists access to the money available to nonprovocative artists to produce their work and to bring it to the public's attention. In a competitive society, the distribution of funds only to those who conform to majority opinion is in effect censorship of minority opinion.[9]

Limiting public funding of provocative art is similar to curtailing academic freedom. In colleges and universities professors are granted tenure, after a period in which they demonstrate their competence, so that they may be free from the pressure of partisan groups to teach and to write about potentially unpopular ideas. Tenure was established not to offer job security to scholars but to encourage the making of new knowledge and to provide for its transmittal to students. Presumably, although the majority of citizens—or a state legislature, a board of regents, or a university president—may oppose at any given time the teaching of a particular idea, in the long run the nation as a whole benefits from an uninhibited exploration of the world. The act that in 1965 established the NEA explicitly protected the NEA from interference from Congress or the public by requiring panels of experts to make the awards: "[T]he advisory panels which shall be composed of highly qualified professionals will give added assurance that government aid does not lead to governmental interference in the practice of performance of the arts" (quoted in Tessier 309).[10] The guiding principle was the same as that of academic freedom: For the good of the public, those most knowledgeable about art would decide what art merited public support.

What is at stake is the freedom of public educational institutions—such as universities, museums, and the NEA itself—to bring to the public recent contributions to the culture's discourse. Helms's suggestion that controversial art look for its support in "the marketplace" may be compared to a requirement that scholars obtain majority approval to proclaim new and potentially disturbing ideas in the classroom or that museums obtain majority approval to mount shows that question widely held religious or philosophical beliefs: In neither case would the public become acquainted with ideas that challenge the established order. Those ideas the public would approve (like the television network programs consumers buy) would be those that do not disrupt. Such a system would perpetuate the political status quo.

Helms would like for the arts what Bennett would like for the humanities: a dualist relationship with the "real world" in which the arts and humanities, supported by the NEA and the NEH, would preserve and transmit the culture's traditional values, educating the American people to the official version of their civilization's past, refining their taste, and reviving their pride as a nation. In this model, the arts and humanities are considered free of ideology, because they do not disturb the established social order. When Samuel Lipman, publisher of *The New Criterion* and a critic of the NEA, angrily linked the NEA's support of the Mapplethorpe exhibit with "multiculturalism"—which he defined as "a widespread assault on what is variously called Western, or European, or white-dominated, or male-dominated civilization"—and then with affirmative action policies, he acknowledged a fundamental transformation of society. Lipman recognized Mapplethorpe's rejection of typological concepts for sexual appearance and behavior as an expression in the arts of the ideology of the larger political movement, which rejects standard views of Western civilization. For Lipman, a revolution is in progress: Multiculturalism, whose "true heart," he says, is "the frankly instrumental use of culture and art as a device of political consciousness-raising," now threatens "the stability of traditional political institutions" (Lipman 24–26). It threatens the ivory tower.

Lipman is right. A holistic conceptual order, which came about in physics and ecology long before neoconservatives noticed it in the humanities and the arts, does mean revolution. And multiculturalism, affirmative action, and the NEA's support of "cutting edge art" (Lipman 25) are all part of it. The culture's intellectual and artistic life is no longer even theoretically separable from its political life. Affirmative Action has influenced the ideas being developed and transmitted because it has changed the composition of the intelligentsia. If these newly hired intellectuals are imparting to students views that differ significantly from received opinion, their teaching will naturally be construed by traditionalists as "political consciousness raising." And of course it is; that is what teaching does.

But paradoxes abound. It was not only the critique of Western values that broke down the walls of the ivory tower; it was also the neoconservative offensive against the academy. It was William Bennett who, as secretary of education, initiated the criticism of the content of humanities courses, and it was the journalist Charles Sykes who aroused nonacademic citizens to think of academic research as "profscam." And although the neoconservatives accuse cultural holists of politicizing the humanities, the neoconservatives have enlisted the public in their condemnation of intellectuals for holding unpopular opinions. It is the neoconservatives who, by battling to preserve the belief that knowledge is above politics, have demonstrated to the populace the holistic insight that knowledge is socially constructed.

At issue are the questions of what should be taught and who should teach, questions that attract public attention once the academy has ceased to be an ivory tower. Cultural holists, with the assumption that different viewpoints generate different understandings of events, find a multicultural professoriat desirable. Traditionalists, with the assumption that truth transcends politics, think that affirmative action policies (which are being used to achieve diversity among the faculty) run counter to the university's purpose: to assemble the "best" scholars and teachers to preserve, transmit, and expand our civilization's knowledge. Employing a vertical model for evaluating scholars, they believe that universities engaged in preferential hiring of minorities are lowering their standards. To traditionalists, the introduction of such programs as Women's Studies and African-American Studies, whose agenda is finally social change through revisionist scholarship and teaching, represents the take-over of the university by leftist radicals. To cultural holists the programs foster new ways of thinking.

To the extent that humanistic scholarship is revisionary, it becomes an agent for change, as much an agent as science has been in this century. This is precisely what neoconservatives fear. But their perception that revisionist scholarship has been accelerated by the inclusion of women, nonwhites, and non-Westerners in the professoriat is actually a confirmation of the cultural holists' assumption that cultural diversity in those investigating the world means multiple and conflicting assertions of truth. The admission of women, nonwhites, and non-Westerners into the ranks of the learned has provided empirical evidence that traditional accounts of Western civilization have been held in place by the homogeneity of the culture's intelligentsia.

❧ The Neoconservative Backlash

Neoconservatives claim, however, that "multiculturalism" is an ideology in itself, that it is characterized not by a plurality of opinion but rather by a unified opposition to the values that define Western civilization. They regard as an "assault" the cultural holists' questioning of what has been generally accepted as truth in the West. This anti-Western viewpoint has been institutionalized, they say, by the tenuring of 1960s campus radicals, who, according to *Newsweek*, "are gaining access to the conventional weapons of campus politics: social pressure, academic perks (including tenure) and—when they have the administration on their side—outright coercion" ("Taking Offense" 48).[11] In 1990 and 1991, one popular newsmagazine after another carried stories about so-called political correctness; and *The New Republic* devoted its February 18, 1991, edition to "the issue of race on campus" to alert the public to the new academic "orthodoxy."[12]

For neoconservatives, the practice of "multiculturalism" is symbolized by the antiharassment codes that some colleges and universities have established to enforce respect for diversity; these are codes of conduct that aim to curtail speech and action that denigrate minority groups (especially women, non-whites, gays and lesbians, but also the disabled).[13]

For example, the University of Michigan adopted in 1988 a policy "on Discrimination and Discriminatory Harassment," which a U.S. district court ruled unconstitutional in 1989. The policy stated that in "educational and academic centers, such as classroom buildings, libraries, research laboratories, recreation and study centers," persons could be disciplined for

any behavior, verbal or physical, that stigmatizes or victimizes an individual on the basis of race, ethnicity, religion, sex, sexual orientation, creed, national origin, ancestry, age, marital status, handicap or Vietnam-era veteran status, and that

a. Involves an express or implied threat to an individual's academic efforts, employment, participation in University sponsored extra-curricular activities or personal safety; or

b. Has the purpose or reasonably foreseeable effect of interfering with an individual's academic efforts, employment, participation in University sponsored extra-curricular activities or personal safety; or

c. Creates an intimidating, hostile, or demeaning environment for educational pursuits, employment or participation in University sponsored extra-curricular activities.

Antiharassment codes were designed to preserve "civility" on campus—ideally, to diminish animosity related to social prejudices. But they were not to be successful for reasons other than their abridgment of the First Amendment. The increase in reports of racial and sexual harassment on campus may reflect not only an increase in discord but also heightened sensitivity to language on the part of those registering the complaints and hostility from others who feel suddenly disadvantaged by affirmative action policies. Shouting derogatory racial and sexual epithets at individuals who have risen in social rank as a result of civil rights legislation may be the way members of a previously dominant group express their desire to preserve a vanishing order. Restriction of speech, as totalitarian societies have demonstrated, does not eliminate antagonisms whose roots are socioeconomic. The codes reflect an individualist philosophy (to which their multiculturalist designers may not themselves subscribe) for creating a better society by punishing the individuals guilty of speech deemed inappropriate rather than by modifying the system that inclines individuals toward racism and sexism. It is an atomistic tactic to resolve a structural problem.

Furthermore, the authoritarian control of language, whether in the name of "civility" or in the name of "decency," is censorship. And censorship is what the Ayatollah Khomeini's supporters demanded of Viking-Penguin: that they not publish *The Satanic Verses* in paperback because it offends Muslim sensibilities.

The similarity in the University of Michigan's antiharassment policy, supposedly the product of multiculturalist thinking, and Helms's original amendment, which claimed to protect traditional American values, is remarkable. Both documents outlaw in publicly supported places (the university campus, NEA-subsidized exhibitions) the expression of opinion that offends; the major difference is that Helms targets art and the University of Michigan targets speech. Cultural holists, to be consistent with their rejection of authoritarianism, should be as opposed to the one as to the other. Authoritarianism belongs to the hierarchical model for society in which those in power maintain order, the order they like, through oppression. The way to create respect for diversity is to address the causes of social prejudice, not to censor its expression, which is simply an effect.

Right-wing critics of the antiharassment codes, many of whom had liked the Helms amendment, have paraded the codes before the public to elicit support for their many-pronged attack on multiculturalism. Sarcastically labeling as "politically correct" not only the codes but also the expansion of the canon to include previously little-known texts by women, nonwhites, and non-Westerners, the critical analysis of Western ideology, the establishment of women's studies and ethnic studies programs, and the preferential hiring of minorities, they have mocked all kinds of efforts to engender in students an unprejudiced appreciation of human variety.

What the neoconservatives have done, however, is to denounce the methods of some multiculturalists in order to turn the public against the multiculturalists' goal, which is a society where no group suffers oppression. By accusing multiculturalist educators of "indoctrination" (Will 72), a concept many newspaper readers relate to totalitarianism, they encourage the public to associate promotion of diversity in the academy with deprivation of individual liberties. (Their own purpose in teaching the great works—to instill traditional values— the neoconservatives do not describe as indoctrination.) Through anecdotes about mandatory instruction in what George Will scornfully called "officially approved thinking" (Will 72), they have convinced much of the public that free intellectual inquiry in higher education is in danger.

Free intellectual inquiry is in danger, but more from the right than from the left. When equal opportunity laws enabled members of groups traditionally at the bottom of the social ladder to participate in intellectual discourse, those individuals naturally expressed views that differed from the views of the dominant class. The campaign against multiculturalism, therefore, is actually a campaign against policies that have permitted the previously speechless to speak. It is in effect a crusade to suppress a conversation about the social order. Because they cannot stop the conversation, opponents of multiculturalism have caricatured it as an attempt to destroy the foundations of Western civilization. Their success in galvanizing the public may be measured by the frequency with which the phrase "political correctness" appears in cartoons, newspaper columns, and letters to the editor.[14]

To see the racist implications of the crusade, one need only examine what the neoconservatives would substitute for multiculturalism. If the opposite of *multiculturalism* is *uniculturalism*, as it must logically be, then it is obvious that their ideal is a situation in which a single culture predominates. Since the United States is now composed of numerous ethnic populations, preserving the dominance of the culture of our "founding fathers" means perpetuating a hierarchical social order in which only those sharing the values of the "founding fathers" teach. The indignation over the tenuring of 1960s "radicals," among whom are many women and nonwhites, implies that thinkers of that generation should not be permitted to contribute to the intellectual discussion of our time because they don't think the right way—they are not "American" enough. To blame affirmative action policies for the "widespread assault on what is variously called Western, or European, or white-dominated, or male-dominated civilization" is to assert that minority groups profess the wrong values. If only certain ideological groups should be tenured, then what opinions must professors communicate in order to be acceptable?

The absurdity of this reasoning becomes evident when one recalls the justification for tenure: to protect the expression of unpopular opinions. At a time when both leftists and rightists view their opponents as wrongly directed, tenure of academic intellectuals is crucial to the maintenance of uninhibited dialogue.

Neoconservatives cannot stop the criticism of Western values, any more than Helms can stop the production of "indecent" art, but they can do what Helms attempted to do: cut back on financial support for research that challenges the established social order. This is precisely what Sykes proposes in his 1989 book *ProfScam: Professors and the Demise of Higher Education,* where he encourages legislatures to abolish tenure and to reduce financial support for research because "only one academic in ten produces original research of any value" (Sykes

257). The cry that professors are spending too little time teaching and too much time writing, heard frequently in the late 1980s and early 1990s, issues not only from citizens dissatisfied with the quality of education students are receiving in research universities but also from opponents of multiculturalism who dislike the scholarship of the multiculturalists. These critics of the academy would prefer that humanities professors, in particular, spend more time in the classroom than in the library, that they be more occupied with transmitting knowledge than with making it. This would be in keeping with the traditionalist notion of the humanist's mission: to preserve and transmit the Western tradition. And it would be in keeping with Helms's philosophy that taxpayers' money should not subsidize the expression of unconventional or antiauthoritarian ideas. It is a form of censorship.

Reaction to Cultural Evolution

The neoconservative campaign against multiculturalism in higher education is a response to the racial transformation of the population of the United States; it is a backlash against civil rights legislation. Although the opponents of multiculturalism believe that they are attempting to preserve "the best that is known and thought in the world," they are actually struggling to maintain the cultural, racial, and sexual hierarchy that has governed social interaction in the West in the last several centuries. The promotion of diversity threatens their rank on the ladder—their own position in society, the position of their race, and the position of their nation in the world. They are correct in seeing multiculturalist scholarship as an attack on "Western values," for it is an attack on their definition of "the West" and on the ladder model itself. The lesson they are learning is that the women and nonwhites who have acquired power as a result of equal opportunity laws are critical of the conceptual order that once relegated them to low status.

The campaign against multiculturalism arose with the nationalist movement of the 1980s. Both have invoked authoritarianism in service of ideological unity. The call to instill patriotism through a Western-masterpiece curriculum, the support for mandating the Pledge of Allegiance in the schools, and the advocacy of a constitutional amendment to prohibit desecration of the flag were rooted in a belief that an ideological disunity at home was causing a decline in the United States' influence abroad. The supposition was that in order for the United States to recapture the authority in global politics that it had enjoyed at the end of World War II its citizens had to be unified in their "American" values, unified in their confidence in America's superiority over other countries, and patriotic. Operation Desert Storm climaxed the new nationalism by offering proof of America's military dominance; and the "victory" parades welcoming home the troops, which also celebrated the success of American weaponry, were hailed as a sign of America's renewed patriotism. Opposition to the president's policy—that is, opposition to authority—indicated, in the competition model for international relationships, lack of patriotism.[15] A reaction to global cultural evolution, this nationalism, like the neoconservative opposition to multiculturalism, represents a desire to retain a traditional identity.

The clampdown on the National Endowment for the Arts is also a reaction to cultural evolution, especially to the changes underway within the United States in the expression of sexuality. The acceptance by the art world of antiauthoritarian art—homosexual art, in particular—signified to Helms a dissolution of American values. In questioning the culture's typological notions of propriety, Mapplethorpe's photography threatened the social order, just as surely as did multiculturalism, the various liberation movements, and the cultural holists' critique of Western knowledge. To uphold what he took to be the American way of life, Helms sought to restrict the public's access to disruptive ideas.

Authoritarianism is a response to social change. The forces of "mongrelisation" are invariably countered by "apostles of purity" devoted to maintaining the familiar order of things. Thus the right-wing backlash to the social transformation of American society in the late twentieth century was inevitable. However, in the long run, the effort to preserve the West's—specifically, the United States'—traditional identity is doomed to failure. The concept of Western civilization over which neoconservatives and cultural holists are battling now will be decided not by the momentary persuasiveness of either side's arguments but rather by the racial and cultural composition of the population. And although neoconservatives may attempt to suppress the voice of academic cultural holists, they cannot prevent the worldwide contact and intermingling of cultures and races, the interaction of peoples with diverse views and interests, the exchange of ideas of justice. That intermingling will bring the ladder down.

In short, a land ethic changes the role of Homo sapiens *from conqueror of the land-community to plain member and citizen of it. It implies respect for his fellow-members, and also respect for the community as such.*

—Aldo Leopold, "The Land Ethic," 1949

6 ❧ Environmentalism

Aldo Leopold was professor of game management at the University of Wisconsin when he wrote the now famous meditation upon nature's processes called *A Sand County Almanac,* published in 1949, a year after his death. Its concluding essay, "The Land Ethic," was to become the cornerstone of environmental ethics.

Leopold opened his essay with the observation that in the course of the past 3,000 years human ethics has evolved. Describing an *ethic* as "a limitation on freedom of action in the struggle for existence" (Leopold 202), Leopold argued that ethics rests upon the premise that "the individual is a member of a community of interdependent parts" (Leopold 203). In fact, ethics may be thought of as "a kind of community instinct in-the-making" (Leopold 203). Since the time of Odysseus, who hanged his slave-girls for their apparent misbehavior during his long absence, Leopold wrote, our concept of the community has broadened. Although Odysseus's contemporaries would not have seen his action as wrong, because the slave-girls were Odysseus's property, three millennia later we find his behavior intolerable. At the end of the twentieth century we believe that our ethical structure should encompass all humans.[1]

Leopold went on to observe that we treat our land much the way Odysseus treated his slave-girls—that is, according to what is most expedient for us. With predominantly economic criteria for determining the value of anything, we have failed to appreciate land as a biotic community of which humans are part; and in our conservation policies we have ignored those elements of nature that do not benefit us directly and obviously. We have viewed land as property, external to our human community, to be conquered and to be used. However, once we recognize *land* as not merely soil but "a fountain of energy flowing through a circuit of soils, plants, and animals" (Leopold 216), we shall form an "ecological conscience" and take responsibility for the health of the "biota." Leopold summarized "the land ethic" as follows: "A thing is right when it tends to preserve the integrity, stability, and beauty of the biotic community. It is wrong when it tends otherwise" (Leopold 224–225).[2]

In making the biotic community rather than the human community alone the center of his ethical system, Leopold was elaborating the ethical implications for human behavior of Darwin's concept of nature. Darwin had shown not only that human beings belong to the animal kingdom but also that all elements of nature evolve in relation to each other. In the "tangled bank" the birds, the bushes, the insects, and the worms, as well as the soil, the water, and the air, are all interdependent. Once we recognize this symbiosis, we discover that our present economic, technological, and philosophical strategies for human prosperity are not only inadequate to achieve human prosperity universally but also detrimental to the land on which human survival depends.

The Domination of Nature

The model Leopold rejected, in which *Homo sapiens* is "conqueror of the land-community," had made possible the scientific and industrial revolutions which established habits destructive of nature. As we have seen, the model was rooted in the philosophy of Plato and Aristotle, but it was held in place by Western religion: by the belief, articulated in Genesis 1, that God had granted humans dominion over nature. In a celebrated essay titled "The Historical Roots of Our Ecological Crisis," first published in *Science* in 1967, the historian Lynn White traced modern attitudes toward nature to Judeo-Christian theology. White attributed our anthropocentrism to the biblical myth that "a loving and all-powerful God had created light and darkness, the heavenly bodies, the earth and all its plants, animals, birds, and fishes" for the sake of human beings, and then had created humans in his own image. Humans shared God's transcendence over nature (White 25).

The great thinkers of the seventeenth century—particularly Bacon and Descartes—developed their rigorous methodology for investigating nature from within this model. Interpreting Genesis as a mandate to the new scientist, Bacon wrote that the scientist's purpose was "to establish and extend the power and dominion of the human race itself over the universe," so that the human race might "recover that right over nature which belongs to it by divine bequest" (Bacon 4: 114–115). Through Bacon's language, even more clearly than through the language of the Bible, we can see the implications for our environment of the human/nature dualism.

Bacon described the scientific project in imagery of torture:

> For like as a man's disposition is never well known or proved till he be crossed, nor Proteus ever changed shapes till he was straitened and held fast; so nature exhibits herself more clearly under the trials and vexations of [mechanical] art than when left to herself. (Bacon 4: 298)

To acquire medical knowledge, scientists must examine the workings of animal bodies, Bacon explained, and so in his utopian fiction *The New Atlantis*, he imagined a zoo

> of all sorts of beasts and birds, which we use not only for view or rareness, but likewise for dissections and trials; that thereby we may take light what may be wrought upon the body of man. . . . We try also all poisons and other medicines upon them, as well as chirurgery as physic. (Bacon 3: 159)

Carolyn Merchant, analyzing Bacon's imagery of sexual conquest in her book *The Death of Nature*, has shown how Bacon conceived of man and nature (like man and woman) in a relationship of opposition. The assumption that human beings, endowed with souls, were outside nature and superior to it made nature seem something the scientist not only could examine but also could manipulate. Bacon was instrumental in formulating science as a search for knowledge through experimentation; in his approach to nature, Merchant says, he was pivotal in the establishment of the technological view: that nature was to be exploited for the material benefits it could provide human beings.

Descartes reinforced the human/nature dualism in his dichotomy of *res cogitans* and *res extensa*. The latter category included all of nature, everything but God and the human mind, or soul. The mind, according to Descartes, is indivisible and therefore greatly different from the body, which, being part of nature, is divisible; nature functions like a machine, and so does the human body, in which the soul resides (Descartes 196). For Descartes, the possession of consciousness distinguishes humans from animals and enables humans alone to experience pain; soulless animals, whom he compared with clocks, cannot feel pain.[3] Cartesian scientists of the period, performing vivisections on dogs in order to understand the circulation of the blood, likened their cries to "the noise of a little spring that had been touched" (Regan 5, quoted from the writings of one of Descartes's contemporaries).

Bacon and Descartes established new ways of interacting with nature. Bacon proposed, in *The New Atlantis*, that nature could best be studied in separate laboratories dedicated to the separate aspects of nature: weather, diseases, minerals, plants, fish, birds, and beasts. Descartes and later Newton mapped out a universe of inert matter, which, because it was made up of particles that interacted according to the laws of mechanics, could be analyzed by attention to its constituent parts. Descartes's rules for empirical research—divide a problem into parts and then proceed from knowledge of the simplest to knowledge of the most complex—became the basis for the methods of much of modern science.[4]

The Cartesian conception of reality was thus mechanistic and atomistic; it generated mechanistic and atomistic ways of knowing and behaving. The clock analogy turned into a powerful metaphor for physicists and biologists of a universe that functioned at every level according to physical laws. Later the steam engine inspired explanations for the earth's geologic processes. The earth appeared to be a "well-oiled machine," writes Daniel Botkin, with replaceable parts, the capacity to keep operating, and the ability to maintain a steady state (Botkin 105). The atomistic character of this model precluded the recognition that the destruction of any single component of nature affected other components in potentially irreversible ways. Conceiving of the earth as a place populated by a multitude of independently created species of animals and plants, whose soil, water, and air were permanent features of it, our predecessors logically assumed that our use of any of the earth's parts could only benefit us. We simply needed to learn how to make nature work to our advantage.

The Appreciation of Nature

After Darwin discredited the dogma of types, we could begin to understand nature as a living, evolving system that includes us humans, an ecosystem in which energy flows through soils, plants, animals, water, and air.[5] We see now that our interference in any aspect of an ecosystem affects the whole. In short, we have discovered that our use of nature for our immediate benefit may ultimately be to our detriment: By focusing on our own well-being alone, we have, paradoxically, endangered our survival as a species.

Twentieth-century environmentalism represents a fundamental challenge to our traditional dualist relationship with nonhumans and with our environment. It is not a coincidence that an environmentalist conscience develops at the same time as feminism, the civil rights movements, and national liberation movements around the world. These movements all reject the model of dominance, whereby, in the spirit/matter dualism that established and ranked opposites, the supposedly superior was justified in oppressing the inferior. At their best, they seek not to reverse the ranking but to put into place a new conceptual order in which relationships may be characterized not by domination but by cooperation. A *web* may be an appropriate metaphor for this new conceptual order, replacing the metaphor of the ladder—a web of four dimensions (because the order evolves in time), the whole of which is affected by the health of all its parts. In such an order cooperative relationships enhance the survivability of all the components of the whole.

Although our environmentalist conscience is a sign that holistic thinking is gradually replacing the human/nature dualism, the hierarchical order of value, and the atomistic model of nature, modern environmentalism itself reflects the competing ideologies of the old model and the new. The anthropocentric environmentalists seek to preserve nature for the good of the human species; the "ecocentric" environmentalists hope to establish a nature-centered ethic. The environmentalists who are philosophically individualistic oppose those who are philosophically ecocentric and holistic. The ecologists who believe that at the planetary level the earth is relatively homeostatic oppose those who believe that it is not. Thus the old thematic oppositions—of human and nature, of individual and community, of stasis and flux—that have shaped Western discourse for over two millennia shape the late-twentieth-century scientific and philosophical discussion of the relationship of human beings to nonhuman nature.

The debates over animal liberation and environmental preservation illustrate the functioning of these dialectics in the transformation of our conceptual order. So that we may see clearly the issues at stake, I am focusing upon the arguments of a half-dozen thinkers, thinkers who are both well respected and polemical, who with their books have sparked controversy among scientists, philosophers, and environmentalists.

❦ Animal Liberation

As the environmentalist philosopher J. Baird Callicott says, the debate about "animal liberation" is actually triangular, with participants from three camps: those hostile to the idea of offering nonhumans moral considerability; those wishing to extend the moral considerability we have previously reserved for humans to some nonhuman animals; and those, like Callicott himself, who address the question ecocentrically. The first group, for the most part, embodies the traditional Western values inherent in spirit/matter, human/brute dualism, but the second and third do not. Though both of them criticize the traditional exploitative model, they themselves express two conflicting philosophical views, one atomistic and the other holistic.

The British scientist Richard Ryder, who has published two books on the rights of "nonhuman animals," judges himself to be a nonanthropocentric environmentalist.[6] He has criticized the exclusive concern for our own well-being as *speciesism*, a term he coined in 1970[7] to mean "the widespread discrimination that is practised by man against the other species" (Ryder, *Victims* 16). He intended speciesism to be seen in relation to racism, he wrote in 1975, because both forms of prejudice indicate an underestimation of the similarities between those discriminating and those discriminated against, as well as a selfish disregard for the interests of others.[8] Because *anti-speciesism* signifies a perception that other animals are our evolutionary kin, it is "an expansion of the family circle," not unlike the expansion envisioned by other liberation movements, where the increased knowledge of others has led to increased sympathy (Ryder, *Animal Revolution* 317).

Ryder's argument that nonhuman life should be protected "universally" rests on the proposition that "species alone is not a valid criterion for cruel discrimination" (Ryder, *Animal Revolution* 3, 6). All "sentients" are capable of suffering; therefore, wherever it is wrong to inflict pain upon a human animal, it is "probably" wrong to do so upon a nonhuman. Since we would not mistreat infants and the mentally handicapped, we should not mistreat nonhumans on the basis of their lower intelligence (Ryder, *Animal Revolution* 8).

In *Victims of Science: The Use of Animals in Research*, Ryder rebuts the argument usually made for medical experimentation on animals, that the whole human race profits from the knowledge acquired through vivisection and drug testing. Pointing out that this was the same argument made by the Nazis for their experiments on Jews, Ryder finds unacceptable the assertion "that the pain suffered by conscious creatures of one species is justified by benefits experienced by conscious individuals of *another* species because the latter species is better than the former" (Ryder, *Victims* 20). Not being a speciesist, Ryder admits no difference between the argument of the medical experimenters and that of the Nazis. "If the pain felt by any individual is to be justified," he says, "it can only be in terms of the benefits accruing to that *same* individual" (Ryder, *Victims* 19).

In the early 1980s the American philosopher Tom Regan published *All That Dwell Therein*, directed at the general public, and *The Case for Animal Rights*, directed at scholars. In the latter book, a lengthy argument for the inherent value of nonhuman animals, Regan proposes a *subject-of-a-life criterion*:

individuals are subjects-of-a-life if they have beliefs and desires; perception, memory, and a sense of the future, including their own future; an emotional life together with feelings of pleasure and pain; preference- and welfare-interests; the ability to initiate action in pursuit of their desires and goals; a psychophysical identity over time; and an individual welfare in the sense that their experiential life fares well or ill for them, logically independently of their utility for others and logically independently of their being the object of anyone else's interests. (Regan 243)

Those who satisfy this set of criteria have inherent value and ought therefore to be treated with respect. The "respect principle" is egalitarian and nonperfectionist, Regan writes. "It enjoins us to treat *all* those individuals having inherent value in ways that respect their value" (Regan 248). He says that vegetarianism is "obligatory" because the eating of meat treats "individuals with inherent value in ways that are inconsistent with the respect they are due"; it violates their rights (Regan 344). Regan thus shifts the emphasis in his philosophical exposition away from human attitudes, implied by the terms *speciesism* and *anti-speciesism*, to the rights of the individual nonhuman animals themselves.

The concept of speciesism is necessarily post-Darwinian. As long as a spirit/

matter dualism distinguished humans from brutes on the bases of our being the sole possessors of reason and our having been created in God's image, the privileging of humans would not have been subject to criticism. God had made us special, according to orthodox belief: God had endowed us with a soul, putting us above nature. However, once Darwin had shown our evolutionary kinship with the animals we had formerly considered to be absolutely distinct from ourselves, then we were bound, at some point in time, to view our relationship with them as exploitative. Animal liberationists consider the extension of rights to our nonhuman relatives to be a moral obligation, on the basis of our being "the same" in the ability to experience pain and pleasure. Because "rights" accrue to individuals, in the Western model, animal liberationists generally conceive of this obligation as one to individuals.

The respect for nonhuman animals signified by the "expansion of the family circle" has led other thinkers to a more fundamental revolution in ethics. If we recognize the value of nonhuman animals, they ask, should we not recognize the value of the ecosystem to which all animals belong?

ꙮ Ecocentrism

Although the animal rights movement may appear to be in accord with an environmental ethic, Callicott argues that it is not, that the very conception of *rights* belongs to conventional Western moral theory based on the notion of individual autonomy.[9] In his 1980 essay "Animal Liberation: A Triangular Affair," Callicott criticizes what he calls the "hyper-egalitarianism" of Ryder, Regan, and others who think of animal liberation as a logical development of political liberalism: "today animal rights, tomorrow equal rights for plants, and after that full moral standing for rocks, soil, and earthy compounds, and perhaps sometime in the still more remote future, liberty and equality for water and other elemental bodies" (Callicott 16).[10] He sees the animal rights advocates, whom he calls "humane moralists," as adhering to the same conceptual model as their speciesist opponents, the "moral humanists," who treat nonhumans differently from the way they treat humans; the humane moralists simply establish a different boundary—sentience—for their moral community. Both moral humanism and humane moralism center on the individual.

According to Callicott, Leopold was suggesting an altogether different model in his precept that "a thing is right when it tends to preserve the integrity, stability, and beauty of the biotic community." Leopold's emphasis was on the *biotic community* as a natural system, a system which could be unbalanced, for example, by the preservation of every individual rabbit, deer, or tree. For Callicott, Leopold was genuinely holistic, concerned with the relationships among the components of an ecosystem rather than with the individual components themselves. Callicott attributes this ecocentric vision to the emergence of the discipline of ecology, which treats the landscape not as an aggregate of objects—animal, vegetable, and mineral—but as an "articulate unity" (Callicott 22).[11] With the atomistic model, thinkers construed moral issues as clashes of the rights of competing individuals, each separately pursuing his or her own interests; with the holistic model, however, thinkers may come to construe moral issues in terms of the health of the community as a whole.

Callicott explains *ethical holism* as follows:

> An environmental ethic which takes as its *summum bonum* the integrity, stability, and beauty of the biotic community is not conferring moral standing on something *else* besides plants, animals, soils, and waters. Rather, the former, the good of the community as a whole, serves as a standard for the assessment of the relative value and relative ordering of its constitutive parts and therefore provides a means of adjudicating the often mutually contradictory demands of the parts considered separately for *equal* consideration. (Callicott 25)

And he defines *ecocentrism* as "a shift in the locus of intrinsic value from individuals (whether individual human beings or individual higher 'lower animals') to terrestrial nature—the ecosystem—as a whole" (Callicott 3–4).

In making the community, rather than its individual constituents, the touchstone for ethical decisions, ethical holists develop a set of priorities significantly different from that of rights advocates. For example, if diversity contributes to the stability of a particular ecosystem, then specimens of rare and endangered species may be given preferential treatment over individuals of larger, globally distributed populations, even if those individuals are psychologically complex sentients, even if they are furry and cute. Oceans, lakes, woodlands, and wetlands are assigned greater value than the individuals living in them. If there is an overabundance of deer in an area, hunting may be appropriate to restore an ecological balance. Meat eating "may be more ecologically responsible than a wholly vegetarian diet" (Callicott 35); in fact, says Callicott, worldwide vegetarianism could be ecologically catastrophic.

Callicott does not dismiss the concerns of the animal rights activists, however. He finds the factory farms that produce meat for supermarkets as morally repugnant as they do, but for a different reason: Factory farms, like research laboratories engaged in vivisection, transform living things from an organic to a mechanical mode of being. The suffering of agribusiness and research animals, which Ryder, Regan, and a host of others protest, is not greater than that of animals living in the wild, who are subject to predation, disease, starvation, and cold. What is immoral is "the transmogrification of organic to mechanical processes" (Callicott 35). So Callicott advocates not vegetarianism but the consumption of food produced organically rather than by machines and chemicals.

In a 1988 essay, "Animal Liberation and Environmental Ethics: Back Together Again," Callicott attempts to find common ground between the animal liberationists and the environmental ethicists, and he does so in the philosophy of Mary Midgley. Midgley has proposed that we think of humans and animals as composing *mixed communities*, since we form social bonds with the dogs, cats, and other domesticated animals with whom we share our lives. This conception provides an escape from the dilemma of either human/brute dualism or egalitarianism extended atomistically to all sentients; it is holistic in that it presents the relationship of human and nonhuman animals as a system. From Midgley's viewpoint, in keeping with Callicott's, the development of factory farms and animal research laboratories means a betrayal of the animals who have been long-standing members of our communities.

Midgley's idea of the mixed community enables us to distinguish between our treatment of wild animals and our treatment of domestic animals. Domestic animals, according to the "Midgley–Leopold biosocial moral theory," as Callicott names it, ought to enjoy the rights and privileges attendant upon their membership in mixed communities; wild animals must be considered in terms of the ecological balance of the biotic communities to which they belong. The fundamental operating principle of an environmental ethic, according to Callicott, is that all members of a biotic community, in their appropriate numbers, ought to be allowed to function in their coevolved life ways. No organism exists outside the natural cycle through which energy flows—and energy flows "from stomach to stomach." Since all organisms eat and are eaten, "whatever moral entitlements a being may have as a member of the biotic community, *not* among them is the right to life" (Callicott 57).

The debate between the animal rights activists and the ecocentric environmentalists is of interest to us because it illustrates the persistence of the atomistic habit of thought in discussions that arise out of holistic insights. Darwin's evidence for the "descent of man" from nonhuman ancestors effectively broke down the dualist distinction between human and brute, enabling thinkers to perceive human and nonhuman animals as one enormous family. The animal rights activists, wishing to bring nonhuman sentients into the moral community, derive a moral relationship from Darwin's demonstration of the common ancestry of humans and brutes. So they extend down the ladder certain "rights"—to consideration, to respect, and to life—which humans have traditionally granted only to humans, and not always to all humans. Their demand for the liberation of the sentients whom we humans have dominated appears at first glance to be a radical rejection of the spirit/matter dualism by which we once differentiated ourselves from nonhuman animals, and therefore a laying down of the ladder. But actually they have not abandoned the traditional Western model, for they continue to use the class criterion—of sameness—for their atomistic granting of rights; they have simply translated "spirit" into the capacity to suffer.

That atomistic conception of rights characterizes another effort born of the expansion of our moral community: the preservation of endangered species. Concern with the preservation of ecosystems in the last few decades, combined with the acknowledgment that we are rapidly diminishing the earth's biological diversity, has produced such legislation as the Endangered Species Act, which has served for two decades to rescue those particular species that scientists have declared almost extinct. Both anthropocentric and ecocentric environmentalists have supported the implementation of this law, perceiving our rampant extermination of other kinds of life to be unethical. However, as *Time* editorialist Ted Gup points out, its species-by-species approach fails to address the underlying causes of the loss of biodiversity. It would be better, suggests Gup, to focus on entire ecosystems, rather than on single species.[12] Gup would agree with Callicott that a holistic policy, one treating the individual species not as autonomous units but as components of biotic communities, would better serve our planet and ourselves. After all, species evolve in relation to each other. As Darwin wrote, extinction goes hand in hand with natural selection (Darwin, *Origin*, 1st ed. 172).

🕭   The Holistic Model

Callicott founds his environmental ethics on a nonatomistic, nondualistic, and nonanthropocentric conception of nature. In a 1986 essay titled "The Metaphysical Implications of Ecology," he compared Leopold's description of nature—"a fountain of energy flowing through a circuit of soils, plants, and animals"—to that of biophysicist Harold Morowitz, who characterizes living things as "dissipative structures," which do not endure in and of themselves but only as the result of the continual flow of energy in the system.[13] Callicott labels the ecosystem model "the field theory of modern biology" because he sees it as conceptually complementary to the paradigm emerging in physics. Ecology, like modern physics, generally treats the system as primary, reversing the traditional subordination of relationships to the individual; its premise is that within an ecosystem relationships determine the function of organisms. A species obtains its character from its adaptation to a particular niche in the ecosystem. Nothing is permanent in nature; nothing is static.

Callicott predicts that this relational view of the individual or self will transform ethics (in Kenneth Goodpaster's phrase) "from egoism to environmentalism" (Callicott 114).

The transformation has already taken place in "deep ecology." In the 1970s the Norwegian philosopher Arne Naess coined the term *deep ecology* to signify an ecocentric understanding of nature. He differentiates "deep ecology" from "shallow ecology," which he considers an anthropocentric environmentalism in its separation of humans from their environment and its evaluation of nonhuman beings and things according to their instrumental value. The shallow ecology movement, because it aims to preserve nature for "the health and affluence of people in the developed countries," Naess says, perpetuates the "master–slave" model implicit in Cartesianism (Naess, *Ecology* 28). The deep ecology movement, however, by viewing humans in the context of the biosphere, inspires a noninstrumentalist, nonanthropocentric ethic, an ecological consciousness.[14] Naess argues for a "biospherical egalitarianism" based not on a "man-in-environment image" but on a nonanthropocentric "relational, total-field image" (Naess, *Ecology* 28).[15] Callicott situates himself in this mode of thinking, which we might more accurately describe as philosophically "inclusivist" rather than "egalitarian."

The "relational, total-field image" of the community is an image of connectedness, what holists would see as "cooperation." In the "field" the diverse members of the community "cooperate" with each other in multiple ways, defining by their interaction each other's function. In the holistic model, *cooperation* does not mean a relinquishment of an organism's supposed original autonomy, as it does in the atomistic model; instead, it means interdependence, the natural relationship of organisms to each other in an ecosystem. Thus, in the holistic model, in which "autonomy" is inconceivable, cooperation is an effect. In other words, *cooperation* is simply a description of the way all systems work. Nineteenth-century evolutionists were generally slow to understand cooperation in nature because they had inherited an atomistic way of thinking about phenomena.

Because most ecosystems are marked by diversity, an ecocentric morality, while not privileging the well-being of the individual over that of the collective, entails an appreciation of difference. Sameness, or membership in a special class, is not a determinant of an individual organism's value; its relationship to the whole is. Ecologist Frank Golley advocates the evaluation of worth according to the vital needs of both the individual (of any species) and the ecosystem. Taking as fundamental the "unity of life and nonlife in a widening circle of relationship, leading ultimately to the planet and the universe" (Golley 55), Golley argues that to maintain life we must maintain, in a predictable state, the system in which an individual has evolved and developed. We humans have the right to satisfy our "vital needs," for which we necessarily kill some other living beings, but we do not have the right to dominate and exploit other species or cause their extinction.

It is the environmentalists' attention to the system that has brought on attacks against environmentalism as a leftist movement, a drive to deprive the individual of freedom. From the viewpoint of traditional moralists the call for environmental protection where such protection does not immediately and obviously benefit humans represents a challenge to the rights of the individual—that is, the rights of the human individual. To them, environmentalism means a subordination of the individual to the community, this time the "land-community." And within the atomistic model the privileging of the community over the individual does indeed signify constraint; it is an infringement on individual liberty; it looks like communism. Moreover, in a capitalist society, in which individual well-being is presumed to depend upon successful economic competition, legislation protective of other species looks like legislation disadvantageous to humans because it reduces profits. It is only within the ecosystem model that a "land ethic" appears advantageous.

Within the ecosystem model, where individual well-being appears to depend upon the community's functioning, the natural goal of its citizens is to make the system work well. Holistic ethics therefore centers more on the individual's social responsibility than on his or her civil rights. The time may have already come when the ideology of individualism no longer benefits individuals, either spiritually or economically. Odum points out that, if we continue to restrict law and ethics to promoting the individual's welfare only, we will overstress the biosphere that enables us to live. If and when we recognize this danger and reorient our law and ethics to acknowledge the value of our species as a whole, other species as well, and our environment, then we shall have healthier "life-support systems," to the benefit of all living things (Odum 270–271). As population growth, worldwide food shortages, epidemics, and environmental pollution make obvious the necessity for intentional cooperation among individuals, among cultures and nations, and between humans and our nonhuman environment, cooperation will appear advantageous to all parties. Then cooperation in cultural relationships, as in biological relationships, will be an effect of the struggle to survive.

❧ Homeostasis and Flux

Among contemporary thinkers who conceive of nature nonatomistically, a debate has erupted over the concept of the earth's "homeostasis," a debate which has major scientific, philosophical, and environmental implications. Although the issue has attracted many participants, it may be enlightening to focus on the arguments of John Lovelock of England and Daniel Botkin of the United States, because they represent positions that can be construed as, at least in one aspect, philosophically opposed to each other. Both of these well-respected scientists have sought and reached an audience for their ideas beyond the scientific community.

Lovelock, in a 1979 book called *Gaia: A New Look at Life on Earth*, hypothesizes that the earth functions as an organism. Objecting to the conventional notion that life adapted to planetary conditions, and that life and the planet evolved in separate ways, Lovelock writes:

> [T]he entire range of living matter on Earth, from whales to viruses, and from oaks to algae, could be regarded as constituting a single living entity, capable of manipulating the Earth's atmosphere to suit its overall needs and endowed with faculties and powers far beyond those of its constituent parts. (Lovelock 9)

He calls this living entity "Gaia," the name the ancient Greeks gave the earth.

Lovelock believes that the only logical explanation for the peculiarity of the earth's atmosphere, whose development is difficult to account for in terms of lifeless planetary processes alone, is the interaction of organisms. In other words, life has transformed the atmosphere and the oceans, and life maintains this transformed environment in a steady state. The atmosphere is an extension of the biosphere, and Gaia is a complex entity comprising the earth's biosphere, atmosphere, oceans, and soil, the totality constituting a feedback system "which seeks an optimal physical and chemical environment for life on this planet" (Lovelock 11). The biosphere is therefore "homeostatic."[16] The sun provides the system's energy.

Lovelock's model is profoundly holistic, profoundly nonindividualistic and nonanthropocentric. Lovelock says:

> Life on this planet is a very tough, robust, and adaptable entity and we are but a small part of it. The most essential part is probably that which dwells on the floors of the continental shelves and in the soil below the surface. Large plants and animals are relatively unimportant. They are comparable rather to those elegant salesmen and glamorous models used to display a firm's products, desirable perhaps, but not essential. The tough and reliable workers composing the microbial life of the soil and sea-beds are the ones who keep things moving, and they are protected against any conceivable level of ultra-violet light by the sheer opacity of their environment. (Lovelock 40)

Although the theory of an interactive relationship between the biosphere and the atmosphere is by now uncontroversial, Lovelock's personification of the earth as Gaia has earned him considerable criticism from ecologists, most of whom cannot accept his metaphorical equation of the biosphere with an organism. They find Lovelock's language mystical and teleological, despite Lovelock's repeated assertion that the universe has no purpose.[17]

Some environmentalists are perturbed by Lovelock's hypothesis that Gaia is homeostatic and consequently resilient, capable of recovering from the ingestion of a variety of "pollutants" poisonous to humans. To Lovelock, the very concept of pollution is anthropocentric and possibly "irrelevant in the Gaian context" (Lovelock 110). Odum, who is not antagonistic to Lovelock, reminds us that even if this were the case, even if Gaia survived a human-made catastrophe such as nuclear war or toxification of the oceans, we humans might not. The resilience the biosphere has exhibited in recovering from globally catastrophic events in past ages should not make us complacent about our current life-support systems (Odum 62).

The Gaia hypothesis is in accord with the deep ecologists' "total-field" conception of nature, in which humans are "just one constituency among others in the biotic community, just one particular strand in the web of life, just one kind of knot in the biospherical net" (Fox 194). In Lovelock's vision there appears to be no remnant of the Aristotelian ladder metaphor, in which some organisms rank higher than others; no Platonic dualism, not even a dichotomy between life and nonlife; no atomism. His notion of stasis is not applicable to any species, only to the planet's ecosystem itself, whose long-term tendency toward equilibrium must be understood in geological time.

Yet even the idea of planetary homeostasis may be related to what Botkin calls an "ancient theme of nature" (Botkin 8), in his 1990 book *Discordant Harmonies: A New Ecology for the Twenty-first Century*. It is the belief that nature, whether conceived of as divinely created, organic, or mechanical, returns to a state of balance and harmony after being disturbed. That belief, Botkin says, is inconsistent with our present knowledge of the earth's evolutionary processes.[18]

In contemporary global ecology Botkin discerns three schools of thought, two of which postulate a "balance of nature." The first, which is compatible with both the divine and the mechanistic conceptions, assumes that nature has a constancy of form and structure that, if undisturbed by humans, will remain indefinitely. The second, compatible with both the mechanistic and the organic, assumes that life creates the constant conditions that it requires, acting like earth's thermostat, as Lovelock believes. The third school, to which Botkin belongs, assumes that the biosphere is always changing and that it is this condition of change that enables life to persist (Botkin 146).

Botkin's basic thesis rests on the proof he assembles that "you cannot turn the biosphere backward from one of its major evolutionary steps to a previous one" (Botkin 149). Climate fluctuations since the earth's formation have brought about irreversible changes in the distribution of life. The transformation of the biosphere occurring as species evolve and become extinct, he argues, is bound to affect the chemical composition of the atmosphere, whose concentration of carbon dioxide has varied since the end of the most recent ice age (Botkin 150). In short, nature (including biosphere, lithosphere, hydrosphere, and atmosphere) is characterized most fundamentally by flux.

Returning at the end of his book to Leopold's aim in conservation, the achievement of "a state of harmony between men and land," Botkin explains that we can reach such "harmony" only if we acknowledge that the character of nature is change. He argues that the awareness that a steady state in the biotic community is *un*natural, anywhere, should lead to the designing of dramatically different wildlife conservation policies from the ones we now have, new policies that allow for change in environmentally protected areas. Since we humans are part of the flux, we must recognize that "nature in the twenty-first century will be a nature that we make" (Botkin 193). Therefore, we must find ways of living that enable the biosphere to function "not only to promote the continuation of life but also to benefit ourselves" (Botkin 191).

This practical anthropocentrism, whose speciesism Botkin would not deny, retains nothing of the traditional dualism of human and nature; it comes out of the knowledge that the universe that is our home is a universe of continuous, purposeless flux, into which the human species fortuitously evolved. For Botkin, that knowledge constitutes an imperative for action. If no God protects our environment, then we humans must. Botkin thus extricates an anthropocentric ethic out of an ecocentric understanding of nature.

Botkin's vision is in keeping with the relativism of contemporary philosophers who postulate a universe without a center in which nothing has intrinsic meaning. It is a universe, as Gould says, of contingency, in which the existence of any species, including our own, is the undetermined, but nonrandom, result of historical events in the evolutionary process.[19] It is a universe in which we humans occupy no privileged position in space-time, but also a universe that we can know only from our particular earthly, human, culturally bound viewpoint. In Botkin's environmental ethics the awareness that human existence is apparently accidental, born of the flux, ought to motivate us to devise ways to thrive in the flux.

Just as Lovelock's Gaia hypothesis has elicited both criticism and enthusiasm, Botkin's book will stimulate spirited discussion. Ecologists are likely to point out that, although change occurs at all levels of the universe, the rate of change differs vastly from the genetic level to the cosmic—rapid, even stochastic and chaotic, at the genetic level of the biosphere but very slow in the atmosphere, hydrosphere, lithosphere, and cosmos. From our human viewpoint, for example, the lithosphere appears relatively stable; ecosystems change slowly, so slowly in some cases that ecologists feel justified in describing them as being in equilibrium; and populations of short-lived organisms change rapidly. When the atmosphere, which we assume ought to be relatively stable, exhibits change perceptible to us in our human lifetimes, then we ought to be alarmed. A description of change, therefore, must take into account the perspective (human) and the time frame. Of course, Botkin would not dispute this.

On philosophical grounds, Botkin is in good company. So is Lovelock. Botkin's understanding of nature corresponds with the cultural holists' understanding of human society: that stasis is not only unnatural but also unachievable. And Lovelock's idea that the earth comprises a single biotic system, which may be of greater significance than his hypothesis of planetary homeostasis, corresponds with the cultural holists' recognition of a global society.[20]

🍃 Ethical Holism

"Biospherical egalitarianism," "deep ecology," "ecocentrism," and "ethical holism" are all ethical elaborations of the holistic model. Leopold and Callicott are developing as an environmental ethic certain ideas that have emerged in civil rights philosophy: rejection of the notion of a rank order of value, criticism of domination, appreciation of diversity within a system, and acknowledgment of interdependence. Lovelock is conceiving of the planet as a biotic unit, at the same time that economists, sociologists, journalists, politicians, environmentalists, and others are conceiving of the planet as a global cultural community. Botkin shares with cultural holists a vision of flux.

The discourse of environmentalism thus has much in common thematically with the discourse of equal rights. Yet one must be careful in understanding the way in which they are connected. Despite Leopold's ideal of changing our relation to the "land-community" from "conqueror" to "plain member and citizen of it," we humans affect by our presence the world we inhabit. We cannot do otherwise. We manipulate our natural environment in whatever we do, and our environmental protection policies simply stipulate how we manipulate it legally and consciously.

The environmentalist version of ethical holism, as formulated by Callicott, which offers philosophical guidelines for our environmental manipulation, should not be taken to support an authoritarian manipulation of human beings. Authoritarianism, cultural holists would argue, is totally inconsistent with an appreciation of the diverse components of a decentered system; it belongs to the model of dominance. If humans are not to be "conqueror of the land-community," neither should humans, of any group, serve as conqueror of the human community. Ideally, we should all be plain citizens, respectful of each other's interests.

Thus the goal of the cultural version of ethical holism is comparable to that of the environmentalist version: to establish and maintain the integrity, stability, and beauty of the human community. By viewing the civil rights movements not in terms of the atomistic dispensation of rights, formerly reserved for the privileged few, to an enlarged family circle but in terms of a conversion to the holistic model, we can easily see what social inclusivism and environmentalism share. In the holistic model for human interaction the recognition of the value of diverse contributions to the health of the whole means an appreciation of the variety of contributions different individuals and different groups make; and the recognition of the interdependence of a system's constituents means the necessity for cooperation. The well-being of the system requires the well-being of all its parts. Because our system is the whole earth—an "articulate unity" of culture and nature—we humans cannot neglect nonhuman nature if we are ever to bring about a (relatively) stable human community.

If we think of human society not as an aggregate of individuals, a portion of whom require our charity, but as a global system that as it is presently ordered enables some to thrive at the expense of others, we must accept a responsibility to modify the system. Because this global system is a human-nature community, we are likely to establish environmental policies that ideologically mirror our evolving social order. Actually, we are more than likely to do so, for it is our model of reality that will determine those policies. Just as the dualistic, atomistic, and hierarchical model configured imperialism, capitalism, and industrialism during the last 300 years, so will the holistic model configure the West's future societal and environmental relationships.

The West's domination mentality has led to disharmony between the sexes, among the races, and among the world's various cultures; it is depleting life on earth. The ideal of ethical holists of all kinds is to develop ways to live in harmony with each other and with the "land."

❧ A World without Absolutes

From our standpoint at the end of the twentieth century, as we come to understand a world of continuous change, we can view the history of Western thought as a successive discarding of absolutes. From Copernicus we learned that the earth is not the center of the universe. From Darwin we learned that human beings were not specially created by God, that all species, including our own, have evolved and are continuing to evolve by natural selection. From Einstein we learned that space and time are not absolute. Now we glimpse a universe of flux, in which our planet itself is evolving toward a future to which we humans may not belong.

Yet, as we have seen, the model of reality our ancient Greek predecessors developed has been remarkably difficult to escape. The concept of a scale of ascent predisposed us to think of differences in terms of rank on a scale of worth, whose social and economic consequences we continue to experience. The spirit/matter dualism that, before Darwin, distinguished humans from brutes reasserts itself in the distinction between sentients and nonsentients made by the animal rights advocates, who condemn their opponents for anthropocentrism; atomism characterizes the rights activists' species egalitarianism. The belief in a static order of things, discredited for the biological kingdom by Darwin, reappears in the concept of the earth's homeostatic ecosystem.

These apparent inconsistencies within the emerging holism belong to the process of change, a process in which innumerable conflicts in presuppositions, values, and interests lead eventually to ways of thinking and interacting that are more widely beneficial than the old. A new order does not emerge all at once.

A world without absolutes, a world of continuous change, is a world whose evolution—cultural and physical—humans may influence. It is a world, therefore, for which humans have responsibility; and since we humans alone, at this stage, are conscious of how we influence it, we have sole responsibility. However, the loss of faith in an eternal order ought not to leave us in despair, for the hierarchical social systems we developed with that faith did not make for social harmony. In the absence of belief that our world was designed to turn out the way we find it, we may hope to make it better. If all is flux, and we know it, then perhaps we may create social justice.

ᶾᐤ   Conclusion

At the end of the twentieth century a new science is being created; it is the study of chaos. We may trace its origins, writes James Gleick in his book on the subject, to meteorologist Edward Lorenz's creation of "toy weather" on a computer at the Massachusetts Institute of Technology in 1960. What Lorenz discovered, and what various thinkers in other scientific fields have subsequently learned, is that, because of "the Butterfly Effect," predictability is perhaps impossible to achieve in large-scale systems. The Butterfly Effect—"the notion that a butterfly stirring the air today in Peking can transform storm systems next month in New York"—is the nickname for "sensitive dependence on initial conditions," the rapid translation of tiny differences in input into overwhelming differences in output (Gleick 8).[1]

The Butterfly Effect, though originally a mathematical principle, may serve us as a metaphor for the holistic conceptualization of reality. It expresses the idea that in a giant system, a system of space-time whose dimensions are ultimately cosmic, all events are—however imperceptibly—interrelated. On a planetary scale we have begun to recognize the effect of Brazilian deforestation, stimulated by Western society's taste for beef, upon the earth's climate. In the arena of international politics we can see that dependence on oil dictates the particular world order the powerful nations find acceptable; if in the 1980s the United States had developed solar energy as a viable alternate to fossil fuels, would President Bush have taken the country to war with Iraq? What kind of world order would we have if the first automobiles produced had been designed to run on alcohol? If, in Gould's example of "the extreme chanciness and contingency of life's history," comets had orbited slightly differently during the heyday of the dinosaurs, the dinosaurs might still rule the earth (Gould, *Wonderful Life* 280).

Once we begin to think holistically, we notice the Butterfly Effect everywhere. In fact, once we have been introduced to the Butterfly Effect, we cannot *not* see it. From now on, having abandoned any assumption of an ideal order that stabilizes or directs phenomena, we are likely to understand our present state of affairs to be the result of "historical contingency," as Gould would say.[2] The idea of historical contingency, intimately connected with the idea of nature as continuous change, has developed over time, from Darwin through Botkin and

Gould. The power of persuasion it now has signifies the increasing hegemony of holism among Western intellectuals.

We have only begun to think about an ethics correlative to this holistic, relativistic vision. Absolutists have traditionally associated relativism with a relinquishment of social obligation, in the belief that without faith in a God to reward or punish the spirit humans have no moral imperative to take care of each other—that without faith in a God individuals look out for themselves alone. But we can attribute that notion not only to a dualist conception of the self but also to an atomistic construction of experience, whereby an individual's well-being is presumed to be enhanced by the material advantages the individual can gain over other individuals. With a holistic construction, we may assume the opposite, that an individual's well-being depends upon the system.

However obvious that may be now, in the emergence of a global society, those at the top of the ladder addressing problems of the system tend to seek solutions that do not disturb its hierarchy. That is why the United States government favors atomistic approaches, at home and abroad, to poverty, pollution, and oppression; atomism supports the political status quo. In fact, the model of dominance, which justified imperialism, colonization, and slavery, was held in place largely by the institutionalization of an atomistic organization of knowledge: the separation of the disciplines from each other and the separation of intellectual inquiry from political action and from moral responsibility.

Awareness of the Butterfly Effect introduces a new conception of moral responsibility in a world that has become a global community. Morality is defined in the holistic model not simply in terms of behavior toward individuals but also in terms of efforts to maintain a just social system: Consciously to uphold an unjust system, even when behaving "morally" toward other individuals, is immoral. If relationships determine the character and function of the individuals of a system, as our understanding of nature now leads us to think, then the well-being of individuals depends upon the well-being of the whole; and the well-being of the whole in turn depends upon biological and social "cooperation" among individuals.

The lesson of cultural holism is that our health—as individuals, as a society, as a species—depends upon our keeping the whole in mind. We cannot exploit, or neglect, any particular set of individuals and expect our global human community to thrive. Nor can we neglect or exploit unduly our "land," for not only is it environmentally unethical to do so but it is also foolish: Our survival depends on the survival of the variety of organisms that keep the earth's biotic system relatively stable. When we keep the whole in mind, we have laid the ladder down.

Notes

1. The adjective *Western* has generally been used in the late twentieth century to designate regions "steeped in or stemming from the Greco-Roman traditions," as well as "the noncommunist countries of Europe and America" (*Webster's New International Dictionary*). I am using the word to describe attitudes and traditions characteristic of the peoples of Europe and North America. Because I am concerned primarily with the transformation of the West's model of reality in the United States, I am directing this book to an American audience. Therefore, the pronoun *we* means, in most cases, "we Americans."

2. In an essay exploring a holistic conception of reality, environmentalist philosopher Frederick Ferré uses the metaphor of the kinetic theory of gases to describe the atomistic, mechanistic model that has governed Western consciousness. He writes: "In this theory the random agitations of individual molecules, bouncing off one another in vast numbers of chance encounters, produce a steady and reliable pressure on the vessel (or in the inner tube) that is holding the gas. It is an apt metaphor in several ways. (1) It illustrates the tendency of modern mechanistic consciousness to think first about bits and pieces, dividing up subject matters into their smallest parts as a systematic procedure. . . . (2) The molecular metaphor also illustrates the supposed *ontological separateness* of the elements of things that is assumed by the modern mechanistic consciousness. These molecules are conceived as infinitely elastic and wholly nonpenetrating: that is, they bounce off one another, relating always according to their own private natures, never blending or merging. (3) Every member of this population of molecules is in actual or potential abrasive contact with all the other members. The only mode of relating is by *mutual repulsion*. (4) Understanding of the phenomenon is wholly in terms of mathematical formulae. Everything, including the degrees of chance involved, is *quantifiable*. (5) There is *nothing more to the situation* than matter in motion. The intangible, the qualitative, the purposive, is simply not present at the root of things. (6) Everything is predictable in principle. Chance rules, but *out of stochastic turmoil comes rigid order* at another level. It is not mere order; rather, a strong necessity emerges from the interplay of many contingencies" (Ferré 232).

3. In times of international "hostilities," such as the war in the Persian Gulf, opposition develops between self-proclaimed "patriots" and peace activists. This antagonism may be seen as an opposition of nationalism, which is rooted in the atomistic model

of international competition, to internationalism, or "globalism," which arises out of the holistic model whose ideal is international cooperation.

4. Smuts, who was prime minister of South Africa between 1919 and 1924 and then later during World War II, was a segregationist. However, the widespread use of the word *holism* by thinkers who do not share Smuts's political orientation—ecologists, for example—shows that the word was not contaminated by Smuts's racism.

5. *Multiculturalism* is not a synonym for *cultural holism* but rather an aspect of it. In calling attention to cultures that the dominant culture has ignored, multiculturalists promote the appreciation of diversity. *Cultural holism* is a more inclusive term than *multiculturalism*, in that it encompasses environmentalism.

Cultural holism in the academy also manifests itself in interdisciplinary research and teaching that has considerably enlarged the scope of traditional humanistic scholarship. Thus, although academic cultural holists may focus primarily on texts, thereby distinguishing themselves from empirical scientists, I prefer not to call them "humanists" because of our traditional notion of the "humanities." Since the scientific revolution, and particularly in the past hundred years, the humanities have been conceived of in opposition to science. Cultural holists reject such dualism, just as they reject all disciplinary boundaries, because they see all ideas about the world as interrelated. See my book *Reconnection: Dualism to Holism in Literary Study*, which shows how Cartesian dualism positioned literary study in opposition to science. Now, with the cultural shift from dualism to holism, the discipline of literary study is losing its traditional philosophical foundation.

6. Theoretical ecologist Bernard Patten formulates a holistic approach to nature: "Collective life in ecosystems, from individual binary interactions to the whole global biosphere, is a coevolutionary continuum of unbroken wholeness encompassing network mediated cybernetic mechanisms of distributed or diffuse control, implicit in dominant indirect effects, that holistically regulate the life-environment relation. Within any system, the significant determinants of change are global, not local." Patten goes on to say that "the problem of holistic science becomes one of system definition" (Patten 293).

7. Of course, wholes are not self-defining, and all systems are open: It is we humans who identify the wholes in our process of making sense of our world. Furthermore, a holist would not assume that any given "thing" would be part of only one whole, or system, precisely because the definition of the system depends upon the observer. What distinguishes the holistic thinker from the traditional Western thinker is the holist's attending primarily to the functioning of a system's components *in relation* to each other.

8. I have chosen to use the term *inclusivist* rather than *egalitarian* here, because egalitarianism is a concept finally intelligible only in the vertical model; there it counters the conventional order of dominance. However, the egalitarianism of the various civil rights movements is indeed a sign of the shift from a vertical to a holistic

conceptualization of reality. *Egalitarianism* refers to efforts to eliminate social hierarchies founded upon the perception of natural inequalities of inherent worth or ability among human beings; it represents a rejection of the "scale of ascent," a rejection of the model of dominance. In the holistic model, which may be symbolized by a web, *inclusivism* refers to the recognition that a system functions efficiently only by the healthy participation of *all* its components. Inclusivism is incompatible with oppression of any kind, because oppression precludes healthy participation by the dominated. A holistic vision is inclusivist in its appreciation of diversity and respect for difference.

CHAPTER 1. THE LADDER

1. The complete title of White's book is *An Account of the Regular Gradation in Man, and in Different Animals and Vegetables, and from the Former to the Latter*. The passage is quoted in Gould, *Flamingo's Smile* 289–290.

2. Aristotle wrote in *Generation of Animals*: "the animal is a body with soul; the female always provides the material, the male that which fashions it, for this is the power that we say they each possess, and this is what it is for them to be male and female. Thus while it is necessary for the female to provide a body and a material mass, it is not necessary for the male, because it is not within what is produced that the tools or the maker must exist. While the body is from the female, it is the soul that is from the male, for the soul is the substance of a particular body" (Aristotle 1: 1146).

3. Aristotle wrote: "we may infer that, after the birth of animals, plants exist for their sake, and that the other animals exist for the sake of man, the tame for use and food, the wild, if not all, at least the greater part of them, for food, and for the provision of clothing and various instruments. Now if nature makes nothing incomplete, and nothing in vain, the inference must be that she has made all animals for the sake of man" (Aristotle 2: 1993–1994).

4. See Arthur Lovejoy's well-known book *The Great Chain of Being* (1936). Alexander Pope used the phrase "chain of being" to describe nature in *An Essay on Man*. He depicted an unbroken chain stretching through insect, fish, bird, beast, man, angel, and God, in which each being's rank depended on the degree of "sensual, mental pow'rs." Inheriting from Plato and Aristotle the notion of "plenitude" (as Lovejoy named the belief that the universe contained all possible kinds of living beings), Pope declared that the chain represented a "full creation," in which "All are but parts of one stupendous whole." Because this was God's order, to challenge one's rank was to be guilty of Pride. "And who but wishes to invert the laws / Of Order, sins against th' Eternal Cause." Pope ended the First Epistle of the poem with the argument that since humanity cannot know God's plan—that what may appear Evil contributes to the universal Good—we must accept the truth that "Whatever is, is right" (Pope 5–15).

5. In his appendix Nott states that he has substantiated Morton's findings with his own research into the sizes of hats sold to the different races. He then presents the following table, with Morton's figures but his own racial groupings:

Internal Capacity of Brain in Cubic Inches

Races	Internal capacity mean	Internal capacity mean
Modern white races		
Teutonic group	92	92
Plasgic ''	84	
Celtic ''	87	88
Shemitic ''	89	
Ancient Pelasgic	88	
Malays	85	83½
Chinese	82	
Negroes (African)	83	83
Indostanese	80	
Fellahs (modern Egyptians)	80	80
Egyptians (ancient)	80	
American group		
Toltecan family	77	79
Barbarous tribes	84	
Hottentots	75	75
Australians	75	

Source: Gobineau, *Intellectual Diversity* 472.

6. Most of the theories of race advanced during this period developed out of the classificatory system of the taxonomist Carolus Linnaeus. In *Systema naturae*, which he published in 1735, Linnaeus put humans, apes, monkeys, and sloths in a category of quadrupeds of human form. Using skin color as a criterion for ranking—and probably the first to do so—Linnaeus then merged physical and cultural characteristics to define four major human groups: *Homo Europaeus*, white, fickle, sanguine, blue-eyed, gentle, governed by laws; *Homo Asiaticus*, sallow, grave, dignified, avaricious, ruled by opinions; *Homo Americanus*, reddish, choleric, obstinate, contented, regulated by customs; and *Homo Afer*, black, phlegmatic, cunning, lazy, lustful, careless, governed by caprice (Haller 4). The late-eighteenth-century German anthropologist Johann Friedrich Blumenbach, who introduced skull shape as an additional criterion for race classification, distinguished five races. The Cauca-

sian, the Mongolian, and the Ethiopian were the three principal ones, but they were connected to each other by two others: the American, which linked the Caucasian and the Mongolian; and the Malay, which linked the Caucasian and the Ethiopian. Blumenbach ranked the Caucasian highest, in part for being the "most handsome and becoming" (Blumenbach 265) and in part for being "the primitive colour of mankind" (Blumenbach 269). Samuel Morton distinguished twenty-two families and put the Teutonic, of the Caucasian group, at the top and the Alforean (Australian), of the Negro group, at the bottom (Nott and Gliddon 466). Other ethnologists established as many as sixty-three categories, as they recognized more and more the real diversity of human beings in the world.

7. The original passage from Gobineau's *Essai sur l'inegalité des races humaines* is as follows: "Il n'y a pas de peuplade si abrutie chez laquelle ne se démêle un double instinct: celui des besoins matériels, et celui de la vie morale. La mesure d'intensité des uns et de l'autre donne naissance à la première et la plus sensible des différences entre les races. Nulle part, voire dans les tribus les plus grossières, les deux instincts ne se balancent à forces égales. Chez les unes, le besoin physique domine de beaucoup; chez les autres, les tendances contemplatives l'emportent au contraire" (Gobineau, *Essai* 105).

One may notice that Gobineau's translator for *The Moral and Intellectual Diversity of Races* gave a rather loose rendition of this passage, beginning with his translation of the word *peuplade* as "human being" rather than "tribe." Aiming not to provide a literal rendering of the original but rather a text meaningful for an American audience (Gobineau, *Intellectual Diversity* 99), he interpreted the adjective *grossières* (as in "coarse" or "vulgar" tribes) as "lower." In so doing, and in substituting the term "higher aspirations" for Gobineau's *vie morale* ("moral life"), the translator believed that he was clarifying Gobineau's statement. His version reveals his culture's ranking of the spiritual over the material.

8. In 1915, the first volume of Gobineau's *Essai* was retranslated into English (this time with much greater faithfulness to the original) and published in the United States under the title *The Inequality of Human Races*. In an enthusiastic introduction to it, Dr. Oscar Levy called Gobineau a "true prophet," praised Gobineau for "his belief in Race and Aristocracy as the first condition of civilization," and associated him approvingly with Nietzsche, "who has branded our morality as Slave-Morality, and consequently as harmful to good government" (Gobineau, *Inequality* vii–viii). Levy did not foresee Adolph Hitler's use of Gobineau's theory.

9. In *Types of Mankind* Nott and Gliddon wrote: "The laws of God operate not through a few thousand years, but throughout eternity, and we cannot always perceive the why or wherefore of what passes in our brief day. Nations and races, like individuals, have each an especial destiny: some are born to rule, and others to be ruled. And such has ever been the history of mankind. No two distinctly-marked races can dwell together on equal terms" (Nott and Gliddon 79).

10. Strong wrote that the Anglo-Saxon race had contributed two great ideas to civilization: civil liberty and spiritual Christianity. Because these ideas represent "the two great needs of mankind," the Anglo-Saxon "sustains peculiar relations to the world's future, is divinely commissioned to be, in a peculiar sense, his brother's keeper" (Strong 161). "Does it not look as if God were not only preparing in our Anglo-Saxon civilization the die with which to stamp the peoples of the earth, but as if he were also massing behind that die the mighty power with which to press it?" (Strong 165).

11. Strong quotes a paragraph from a late edition of *The Descent of Man*, as follows: "There is apparently much truth in the belief that the wonderful progress of the United States, as well as the character of the people, are the results of natural selection; for the more energetic, restless, and courageous men from all parts of Europe have emigrated during the last ten or twelve generations to that great country, and have there succeeded best" (Strong 170; see Darwin, *Descent* 1: 179.).

12. The black races were often called "the Hamitic peoples," because they were considered to be Ham's descendants. In Genesis, when Noah discovered that his son Ham had looked at his naked body, Noah condemned Ham's son Canaan to servitude. According to the Hamitic legend, the mark of servitude was color.

13. In 1867, in the midst of the controversy over the Negro's voting rights, an anonymous 48-page pamphlet called *The Negro: What Is His Ethnological Status?* was published in Cincinnati. Signed "Ariel," and later attributed to Buckner H. Payne, the essay argued that the Negro did not descend from Adam and Eve, that the Negro was not of the cursed race of Ham but instead was created by God before Adam. Adam, of course, was white. Spinning out a complex interpretation of the Hebrew story of Creation, the author attempted to prove that because God had created no species since the flood, the Negro must have entered the ark "as a beast" (Payne 21); the Negro, therefore, had no soul (Payne 44). In conclusion, "To make the negro, the political, social and religious equal of the white race by *law*, by *statute* and by *constitutions*, can easily be effected in *words*; but so to elevate the negro *jure divino*, is simply *impossible*. You can not elevate a *beast* to the level of a son of God—a son of Adam and Eve—but you may depress the sons of Adam and Eve, with their *impress* of the Almighty, *down to the level of a beast*" (Payne 48). American citizens, he argued, would be committing an offense against God if they were to grant the Negro "equality"; in fact, they should either "send him back to Africa or re-enslave him" (Payne 48).

14. Darwin defined *natural selection* as follows: "As many more individuals of each species are born than can possibly survive; and as, consequently, there is a frequently recurring struggle for existence, it follows that any being, if it vary however slightly in any manner profitable to itself, under the complex and sometimes varying conditions of life, will have a better chance of surviving, and thus be *naturally selected*. From the strong principle of inheritance, any selected variety will tend to propagate its new and modified form" (Darwin, *Origin*, 1st ed. 5).

15. Darwin thought that the diagram of a tree of increasing complexity and diversity represented appropriately both the extinction of species and the evolutionary development of the species presently existing. "Of the many twigs which flourished when the tree was a mere bush, only two or three, now grown into great branches, yet survive and bear all the other branches; so with the species which lived during long-past geological periods, very few now have living and modified descendants" (Darwin, *Origin*, 1st ed. 129). Just as limbs and branches decay and drop off a living tree, enabling the stronger to grow large, so in the course of time have whole families become extinct, leaving no living representatives and making themselves known to us only through fossils.

But why, in the fossil record, do we find so few "transitional links"? In chapter 9 Darwin addressed this question directly, blaming the imperfect geological record for not showing evidence of the enormous number of intermediate species now extinct (Darwin, *Origin*, 1st ed. 280). Because he felt certain that nature "can never take a leap, but must advance by the shortest and slowest steps" (Darwin, *Origin*, 1st ed. 194), Darwin had to hold to his argument that the geological record was incomplete. It was necessarily incomplete, he said, because relatively few organic beings inhabited areas, such as the ocean depths, where their remains could be preserved in masses of sediment capable of withstanding the earth's changes. Furthermore, we should not expect to find fossil forms directly linking living species. Instead, since different species have descended from common but unknown progenitors, we should look for forms intermediate between the species and their common ancestor. In other words, we should seek not fossils linking the horse directly to the tapir but fossils linking each to an unknown common parent. The various branches on the tree are related only through the common limb out of which they grew.

The iconography of the branching tree has recently come under criticism. In his book *Wonderful Life* Harvard paleontologist Stephen Jay Gould argues that the "tree" has suggested to many that life begins with the simple and progresses to more numerous and, by implication, better and better organisms. This tendency to conflate an organism's position in geological time with inherent worth, which we find in interpretations of the evolutionary tree, comes out of the evolutionary ladder model inspired by Aristotle's "scale of ascent." The concept of the ladder also generated the many drawings of the "march of human progress," whose purpose was to show the evolutionary stages through which humans passed on their way from their ape ancestry to their present state. "The familiar iconographies of evolution are all directed," Gould says, "toward reinforcing a comfortable view of human inevitability and superiority" (Gould, *Wonderful Life* 28).

16. At the end of *On the Origin of Species* Darwin wrote: "It is interesting to contemplate a tangled bank, clothed with many plants of many kinds, with birds singing on the bushes, with various insects flitting about, and with worms crawling through the damp earth, and to reflect that these elaborately constructed forms, so different

from each other, and dependent upon each other in so complex a manner, have all been produced by laws acting around us" (Darwin, *Origin*, 1st ed. 489).

17. Darwin explained the human conscience and the belief in God as an effect of evolution: "The moral nature of man has reached the highest standard as yet attained, partly through the advancement of the reasoning powers and consequently of a just public opinion, but especially through the sympathies being rendered more tender and widely diffused through the effects of habit, example, instruction, and reflection. It is not improbable that virtuous tendencies may through long practice be inherited. With the more civilised races, the conviction of the existence of an all-seeing Deity has had a potent influence on the advancement of morality. Ultimately man no longer accepts the praise or blame of his fellows as his chief guide, though few escape this influence, but his habitual convictions controlled by reason afford him the safest rule. His conscience then becomes his supreme judge and monitor. Nevertheless the first foundation or origin of the moral sense lies in the social instincts, including sympathy; and these instincts no doubt were primarily gained, as in the case of the lower animals, through natural selection" (Darwin, *Descent* 2: 394).

18. In *The Descent of Man* Darwin explained imperialism as an effect of evolution: "At the present day civilised nations are everywhere supplanting barbarous nations, excepting where the climate opposes a deadly barrier; and they succeed mainly, though not exclusively, through their arts, which are the products of the intellect. It is, therefore, highly probable that with mankind the intellectual faculties have been gradually perfected through natural selection" (Darwin, *Descent* 1: 160).

19. The story of Marx's offering to dedicate a volume of *Capital* to Darwin is now thought to have been based on a misinterpretation of the correspondence between Marx and Darwin (Bowler 283–284).

20. Spencer coined the term in *Principles of Biology* (1865–67), and Darwin accepted it as a synonym for his term "Natural Selection." In the sixth edition of the *Origin* Darwin wrote: "Owing to this struggle [for life], variations, however slight and from whatever cause proceeding, if they be in any degree profitable to the individuals of a species, in their infinitely complex relations to other organic beings and to their physical conditions of life, will tend to the preservation of such individuals, and will generally be inherited by the offspring. The offspring, also, will thus have a better chance of surviving, for, of the many individuals of any species which are periodically born, but a small number can survive. I have called this principle, by which each slight variation, if useful, is preserved, by the term Natural Selection, in order to mark its relation to man's power of selection. But the expression often used by Mr. Herbert Spencer of the Survival of the Fittest is more accurate, and is sometimes equally convenient" (Darwin, *Origin*, 6th ed. 76–77).

21. Darwin had written that, although children did not have equal opportunity in the race for success since in civilized countries men bequeath wealth to their children,

such inequality was not "an unmixed evil": "without the accumulation of capital the arts could not progress: and it is chiefly through their power that the civilised races have extended, and are now everywhere extending, their range, so as to take the place of the lower races" (Darwin, *Descent* 1: 169).

22. Carnegie loathed and feared communism. He wrote: "for civilization took its start from the day when the capable, industrious workman said to his incompetent and lazy fellow, 'If thou dost not sow, thou shalt not reap,' and thus ended primitive Communism by separating the drones from the bees. . . . To those who propose to substitute Communism for this intense Individualism, the answer therefore is: The race has tried that. All progress from that barbarous day to the present time has resulted from its displacement. Not evil, but good, has come to the race from the accumulation of wealth by those who have had the ability and energy to produce it" (Carnegie 18).

23. Darwin explained in the following passage how natural selection favored humans who cooperated with each other: "In order that primeval men, or the ape-like progenitors of man, should have become social, they must have acquired the same instinctive feelings which impel other animals to live in a body; and they no doubt exhibited the same general disposition. They would have felt uneasy when separated from their comrades, for whom they would have felt some degree of love; they would have warned each other of danger, and have given mutual aid in attack or defence. All this implies some degree of sympathy, fidelity, and courage. Such social qualities, the paramount importance of which to the lower animals is disputed by no one, were no doubt acquired by the progenitors of man in a similar manner, namely, through natural selection, aided by inherited habit. When two tribes of primeval man, living in the same country, came into competition, if the one tribe included (other circumstances being equal) a greater number of courageous, sympathetic, and faithful members, who were always ready to warn each other of danger, to aid and defend each other, this tribe would without doubt succeed best and conquer the other. Let it be borne in mind how all-important, in the never-ceasing wars of savages, fidelity and courage must be. The advantage which disciplined soldiers have over undisciplined hordes follows chiefly from the confidence which each man feels in his comrades. Obedience, as Mr. Bagehot has well shewn, is of the highest value, for any form of government is better than none. Selfish and contentious people will not cohere, and without coherence nothing can be effected. A tribe possessing the above qualities in a high degree would spread and be victorious over other tribes; but in the course of time it would, judging from all past history, be in its turn overcome by some other and still more highly endowed tribe. Thus the social and moral qualities would tend slowly to advance and be diffused throughout the world" (Darwin, *Descent* 1: 161–163).

24. See Mayr, *Animal Species and Evolution* 21, *Toward a New Philosophy of Biology* 527, and *Evolution and the Diversity of Life* 28–29, for a discussion of the "New Synthesis."

Mayr explains that for the populationist, race is based "on the simple fact that no two individuals are the same in sexually reproducing organisms and that consequently no two aggregates of individuals can be the same. If the average difference between two groups of individuals is sufficiently great to be recognizable on sight, we refer to such groups of individuals as different races. Race, thus described, is a universal phenomenon of nature occurring not only in man but in two thirds of all species of animals and plants" (Mayr, *Evolution* 28).

25. The opposition of the humanities to the sciences can be traced back to the early seventeenth century, when Francis Bacon, setting forth rules for the description of nature, distinguished between literature and science on the basis of the spirit/matter dualism. Impatient with the rhetorical style of the ancients, Bacon banned from scientific writing "ornaments of speech, similitudes, treasury of eloquence, and such like emptinesses" (Bacon 4: 254–255). These he reserved for "poesy," which, partaking "somewhat of a divine nature," "raises the mind and carries it aloft, accommodating the shows of things to the desires of the mind, not (like reason and history) buckling and bowing down the mind to the nature of things" (Bacon 4: 316). By separating rhetorical from nonrhetorical language, Bacon not only established a methodological foundation for empirical science, the neutral description of "things," but also articulated a difference between literature and science, which later pitted the disciplines against each other. (See Craige, *Reconnection* 15–18.)

26. Arnold's concept of "humane letters" is more inclusive than our twentieth-century concept of the "humanities" has been. Arnold wrote: "Let us, I say, be agreed about the meaning of the terms we are using. I talk of knowing the best which has been thought and uttered in the world; Professor Huxley says this means knowing *literature*. Literature is a large word; it may mean everything written with letters or printed in a book. Euclid's *Elements* and Newton's *Principia* are thus literature. All knowledge that reaches us through books is literature. But by literature Professor Huxley means *belles lettres*. He means to make me say, that knowing the best which has been thought and said by the modern nations is knowing their *belles lettres* and no more. And this is no sufficient equipment, he argues, for a criticism of modern life. But as I do not mean, by knowing ancient Rome, knowing merely more or less of Latin *belles lettres*, and taking no account of Rome's military, and political, and legal, and administrative work in the world; and as, by knowing ancient Greece, I understand knowing her as the giver of Greek art, and the guide to a free and right use of reason and to scientific method and the founder of our mathematics and physics and astronomy and biology,—I understand knowing her as all this, and not merely knowing certain Greek poems, and histories, and treatises, and speeches,—so as to the knowledge of modern nations also. By knowing modern nations, I mean not merely knowing their *belles lettres*, but knowing also what has been done by such men as Copernicus, Galileo, Newton, Darwin" (Arnold 10: 58–59).

27. Although he urged his fellow intellectuals to become well acquainted with "one great

literature, at least, besides [their] own; and the more unlike [their] own, the better,"
Arnold conceived of literature as essentially European. He wrote in "The Function of
Criticism at the Present Time": "But, after all, the criticism I am really concerned
with,—the criticism which alone can much help us for the future, the criticism
which, throughout Europe, is at the present day meant, when so much stress is laid
on the importance of criticism and the critical spirit,—is a criticism which regards
Europe as being, for intellectual and spiritual purposes, one great confederation,
bound to a joint action and working to a common result; and whose members have,
for their proper outfit, a knowledge of Greek, Roman, and Eastern antiquity, and of
one another. Special, local, and temporary advantages being put out of account, that
modern nation will in the intellectual and spiritual sphere make most progress,
which most thoroughly carries out this programme. And what is that but saying that
we too, all of us, as individuals, the more thoroughly we carry it out, shall make the
more progress?" (Arnold 3: 284).

28. Although it was right that the exceptionally talented individual could rise in rank,
Eliot said, "the ideal of an educational system which would automatically sort out
everyone according to his native capacities is unattainable in practice; and if we
made it our chief aim, would disorganize society and debase education" (Eliot, *Notes*
103).

29. Eliot defined Europe's cultural heritage as Christian, asserting in *Notes towards the
Definition of Culture* that "only a Christian culture could have produced a Voltaire or
a Nietzsche" (Eliot, *Notes* 126), and sought spiritual authority for himself in Anglo-
Catholicism.

30. See Cary Nelson's recent book *Repression and Recovery: Modern American Poetry and
the Politics of Cultural Memory, 1910–1945* for a full account of how the literary
establishment "culturally repressed" the leftist poetry written during the first half of
the twentieth century.

CHAPTER 2. EQUAL RIGHTS

1. In *Complaints and Disorders: The Sexual Politics of Sickness*, Barbara Ehrenreich and
Deirdre English show how upper-class women were considered to be physically very
different from lower-class women. Upper-class women, in the latter half of the
nineteenth century, were viewed as frail, in need of bed rest for menstrual periods,
pregnancy, menopause, and emotional shock. Lower-class women, who as domes-
tics and factory laborers enabled the upper-class women to take to their beds whenever they felt weak, were viewed as inherently robust and therefore capable of
continuous work but also as contaminated with the germs of disease. As Ehrenreich
and English say, "Upper- and upper-middle-class women were 'sick'; working-class
women were 'sickening' " (Ehrenreich and English 14).

2. Briefly, the story of the Birmingham campaign is as follows. In 1962, Birmingham was still fully segregated. Rather than integrate its parks, when a federal court order had banned park segregation, Birmingham had closed them down and given up its baseball team. Blacks were unwelcome in white churches, allowed to buy goods in white department stores but prohibited from eating at their lunch counters, entitled to use only those water fountains and restrooms designated "Colored," systematically denied good jobs, and discouraged from voting. Blacks, who constituted two thirds of the city's population, made up only one eighth of its voters. At a time when Birmingham claimed that its Negroes were "satisfied," its police had failed to bring to justice those responsible for the bombings of seventeen black churches and homes of civil rights leaders. The commissioner of public safety was Eugene ("Bull") Connor, "a racist who prided himself on knowing how to handle the Negro and keep him in his 'place.'" Birmingham, wrote King, was "the country's chief symbol of racial intolerance" (King, *Why We Can't Wait* 41–42, 47).

On April 3, 1963, one hundred years, three months, and two days after President Lincoln had issued the Emancipation Proclamation, King's campaign began, with a boycott of downtown merchants and a series of "sit-ins" at downtown drugstore and department store lunch counters. When the demonstrators refused to leave, they were arrested under the local "trespass after warning" ordinance. According to King, he and the other organizers then held the first of sixty-five nightly mass meetings to "galvanize" the Negro community and to teach nonviolence. They also conducted training sessions in which demonstrators learned "to resist without bitterness; to be cursed and not reply; to be beaten and not hit back" (King, *Why We Can't Wait* 57–60). On April 10, Bull Connor obtained a court injunction directing the SCLC to cease their activities until they had argued in court their right to demonstrate. On April 12, Good Friday, King and Abernathy defied the court order, which they believed was unconstitutional, and led a march, singing freedom songs, from the Zion Hill Church to downtown Birmingham. King and Ralph Abernathy were arrested and placed in solitary confinement, where King wrote his famous "Letter from Birmingham Jail." Eight days later they were released.

On May 2, over a thousand black children, between the ages of six and sixteen, marched downtown from the Sixteenth Street Baptist Church. The police arrested 900 of them. On May 3, Connor ordered his police to block the doors of the same church to prevent the multitude of children jammed inside—again, perhaps a thousand—from leaving it. When they escaped to join the large crowd of demonstrators and onlookers gathered in the park across the street, Connor ordered the police to attack. The police did so with dogs, clubs, and high-pressure fire hoses, which knocked people off their feet and pinned them to buildings. Although a few spectators "not trained in the discipline" retaliated by throwing rocks and bottles, the trained demonstrators remained nonviolent, wrote King (King, *Why We Can't Wait* 106). Television carried this incident to viewers across the nation. As an NBC correspondent said, "Before television, the American public had no idea of the abuses blacks suffered in the South. We showed them what was happening; the brutality, the police dogs, the miserable conditions. . . . We made it impossible for Congress not to act" (quoted in Colaiaco 66). Actually, King and the SCLC had shown the country what was happening. By provoking Bull Connor into using force against unresisting demonstrators, who were asking only for their constitutional rights, they brought the injustice of white supremacy to the attention of television journalists. (For more details of this event, see Colaiaco's *Martin Luther King, Jr.*)

On May 10, with the unasked-for help of Assistant Attorney General Burke Marshall, sent by President Kennedy, Birmingham's business leaders and the SCLC reached an accord.

3. In the Selma campaign of 1965, King outlined the general strategy of militant nonviolence:

1. Nonviolent demonstrators go into the streets to exercise their constitutional rights.
2. Racists resist by unleashing violence against them.
3. Americans of conscience in the name of decency demand federal intervention and legislation.
4. The Administration, under mass pressure, initiates measures of immediate intervention and remedial legislation. (Quoted in Colaiaco 138)

4. In 1882, Friedrich Nietzsche interpreted the scientific discoveries of his times as signifying the death of God. In a parable about a madman seeking God among people unaware of God's absence, Nietzsche wrote: "The madman jumped into their midst and pierced them with his eyes. 'Whither is God?' he cried; 'I will tell you. *We have killed him*—you and I. All of us are his murderers. But how did we do this? How could we drink up the sea? Who gave us the sponge to wipe away the entire horizon? What were we doing when we unchained this earth from its sun? Whither is it moving now? Whither are we moving? Away from all suns? Are we not plunging continually? Backward, sideward, forward, in all directions? Is there still any up or down? Are we not straying as through an infinite nothing? Do we not feel the breath of empty space? Has it not become colder? Is not night continually closing in on us? Do we not need to light lanterns in the morning? Do we hear nothing as yet of the noise of the gravediggers who are burying God? Do we smell nothing as yet of the divine decomposition? Gods, too, decompose. God is dead. God remains dead. And we have killed him.

" 'How shall we comfort ourselves, the murderers of all murderers? What was holiest and mightiest of all that the world has yet owned has bled to death under our knives: who will wipe this blood off us? What water is there for us to clean ourselves? What festivals of atonement, what sacred games shall we have to invent? Is not the greatness of this deed too great for us? Must we ourselves not become gods simply to appear worthy of it? There has never been a greater deed; and whoever is born after us—for the sake of this deed he will belong to a higher history than all history hitherto' " (Nietzsche 181).

5. See John Dewey's essay "The Influence of Darwinism on Philosophy," published on the fiftieth anniversary of the *Origin*'s publication, for a discussion of how "the new logic introduces responsibility into the intellectual life" (Dewey, *Influence of Darwin* 17).

6. The word *ecofeminisme* was coined by Françoise d'Eaubonne in her book *Le Feminisme ou la mort* (1974), pp. 213–252.

For further discussion of ecofeminism, see Karen Warren, "Feminism and Ecology: Making Connections," *Environmental Ethics* 9.1 (1987), and "The Power and the Promise of Ecological Feminism," *Environmental Ethics* 12.2 (1990). Other scholars who have connected the feminist movement with the growth of ecological consciousness are Leonie Caldecott and Stephanie Leland, eds., *Reclaim the Earth: Women Speak Out for Life on Earth* (1983); Jim Cheney, "Eco-Feminism and Deep Ecology," *Environmental Ethics* 9 (1987); Andrée Collard with Joyce Contrucci, *Rape of the Wild: Man's Violence against Animals and the Earth* (1988); Katherine Davies, "Historical Associations: Women and the Natural World," *Women and Environments* 9.2 (1987); Sharon Doubiago, "Deeper than Deep Ecology: Men Must Become Feminists," *New Catalyst Quarterly* 10 (Winter 1987–88); Brian Easlea, *Science and Sexual Oppression: Patriarchy's Confrontation with Women and Nature* (1981); Elizabeth Dodson Gray, *Green Paradise Lost* (1979); Susan Griffin, *Women and Nature: The Roaring inside Her* (1978); Joan L. Griscom, "On Healing the Nature/History Split in Feminist Thought," *Heresies #13: Feminism and Ecology* 4.1 (1981); Ynestra King, "What Is Ecofeminism?" *The Nation*, 12 Dec. 1987; Carolyn Merchant, *The Death of Nature: Women, Ecology, and the Scientific Revolution* (1980); Judith Plant, ed., *Healing Our Wounds: The Power of Ecological Feminism* (1989); Rosemary Radford Ruether, *New Woman/New Earth: Sexist Ideologies & Human Liberation* (1975); Kirkpatrick Sale, "Ecofeminism—A New Perspective," *The Nation*, 26 Sept. 1987; Ariel Kay Salleh, "Deeper than Deep Ecology: The Eco-Feminist Connection," *Environmental Ethics* 6 (1984); Vandana Shiva, *Staying Alive: Women, Ecology, and Development* (1988); Miriam Wyman, "Explorations of Ecofeminism," *Women and Environments* (Spring 1987); Michael E. Zimmerman, "Feminism, Deep Ecology, and Environmental Ethics," *Environmental Ethics* 9 (1987).

CHAPTER 3. CULTURAL HOLISM IN THE ACADEMY

1. Bennett, in his tenure as the nation's secretary of education, entered the 1988 Stanford University curriculum controversy to accuse "leftist" faculty proposing to add non-Western material to Stanford's traditional Western culture courses of depriving

students of an education; his argument was that the West "has set the moral, political, economic and social standards for the rest of the world" (quoted in Atlas 26). He interpreted as a signal of disrespect for "the West" the attempt to include in the Western culture courses the writings of women, persons of color, and non-Europeans. In declaring that the Stanford radicals were "trashing Plato and Shakespeare," Bennett ignored the actual proposal. Originally, the course had required students to read fifteen "classic texts." Now students would read the Old and New Testaments, the works of Plato, Augustine, Machiavelli, Rousseau, and Marx, and texts from "at least one non-European culture," with "substantial attention to issues of race, gender and class" (Atlas 26). For further details of the Stanford curriculum controversy, see Sancton 74–76.

2. In its April 9, 1990, issue, *Time* reported that in 1990 a fourth of Americans were nonwhite and that by the end of the twentieth century, if current trends in immigration and birth rates persist, the Hispanic population of the United States will probably have further increased by 21 percent, the Asian population by 22 percent, the black population by 12 percent, and the white population by little more than 2 percent. By 2056, *Time* predicted, "the 'average' U.S. resident, as defined by Census statistics, will trace his or her descent to Africa, Asia, the Hispanic world, the Pacific Islands, Arabia—almost anywhere but white Europe" (Henry 28).

3. In 1900, President William R. Harper of the University of Chicago summarized as follows the application of the principle of academic freedom: "(1) A professor is guilty of an abuse of privilege who promulgates as truth ideas or opinions which have not been tested scientifically by his colleagues in the same department of research or investigation. (2) A professor abuses his privilege who takes advantage of a classroom exercise to propagate the partisan view of one or another of the political parties. (3) A professor abuses his privilege who in any way seeks to influence his pupils or the public by sensational methods. (4) A professor abuses his privilege of expression of opinion when, altho a student and perhaps an authority in one department or group of departments, he undertakes to speak authoritatively on subjects which have no relationship to the department in which he was appointed to give instruction. (5) A professor abuses his privilege in many cases when, altho shut off in large measure from the world and engaged within a narrow field of investigation, he undertakes to instruct his colleagues or the public concerning matters in the world at large in connection with which he has had little or no experience" (quoted in Dewey, "Academic Freedom" 8–9).

Not only does this paragraph reveal a dualistic distinction between the academic world and "the world at large," which is itself based on a mind/matter dichotomy, but it also reveals an atomistic conception of knowledge. The view that fields of expertise were intrinsically separable from each other, which supported the practice of academic specialization, made possible proviso (4).

4. Roland Barthes explained this terminology in his essay "From Work to Text," first published in 1971. See also his 1968 essay "The Death of the Author." Both are reprinted in Barthes, *Image, Music, Text.*

5. Of course, we daily encounter "signs" whose meaning does seem fixed: a stop sign, for example. However, even a stop sign's meaning is contextual: At a street corner it gives a legal order; in a museum of conceptual art, it does not. See Stanley Fish's explanation for the contextuality of meaning in his essay "Normal Circumstances, Literal Language, Direct Speech Acts, the Ordinary, the Everyday, the Obvious, What Goes without Saying, and Other Special Cases" in *Is There a Text in This Class?*

6. Whorf developed his ideas in relation to those of Edward Sapir, and their theory of language's function in perception has come to be known as the Whorf–Sapir hypothesis. Whorf opened his famous essay, "The Relation of Habitual Thought and Behavior to Language," with the following passage from Sapir's writing: "Human beings do not live in the objective world alone, nor alone in the world of social activity as ordinarily understood, but are very much at the mercy of the particular language which has become the medium of expression for their society. It is quite an illusion to imagine that one adjusts to reality essentially without the use of language and that language is merely an incidental means of solving specific problems of communication or reflection. The fact of the matter is that the 'real world' is to a large extent unconsciously built up on the language habits of the group. . . . We see and hear and otherwise experience very largely as we do because the language habits of our community predispose certain choices of interpretation" (quoted in Whorf 134). In his essay Whorf compared the concepts of time and space given by the Hopi language with those given by SAE (Standard Average European) languages, producing a "linguistic theory of relativity." He concluded that our reality is finally a linguistic construction, as is our science: "Newtonian space, time, and matter are no intuitions. They are recepts from culture and language. That is where Newton got them" (Whorf 153).

7. The recently published two-volume *Heath Anthology of American Literature*, whose general editor is Paul Lauter, may serve well the interests of cultural holists teaching courses in American literature. Already satirized by traditionalists as the "Heath Travesty of American Literature" (McMillen A15), the anthology includes the work of over 300 individuals, of whom 105 are women, 55 are black, and 61 are American Indian, Chicano, or Hispanic. Its section titled "Colonial Period to 1700" presents songs by Zuni, Pima, Hopi, and Iroquois Indians, as well as writings by Christopher Columbus, Alvar Nuñez Cabeza de Vaca, and other explorers. "Regional Voices, National Voices" contains African-American folk tales, as well as texts by Mark Twain, Charles Waddell Chesnutt, Paul Laurence Dunbar, William Dean Howells, Henry James, Kate Chopin, Stephen Crane, and Jack London. "Issues and Visions in Post–Civil War America" contains ghost-dance songs and corridos, as well as texts by Standing Bear, Charlotte Perkins Gilman, W. E. B. Du Bois, Upton Sinclair, and

Henry Adams. Needless to say, many of these authors have not been included in the major anthologies, such as Norton's, which have heretofore defined "the canon."

8. Computers and copiers enable individuals to assemble a wide variety of texts and materials pertinent to their particular interests. By distributing across society the opportunities for the creation and transmission of knowledge, new communications technology makes obvious the process of the construction of knowledge; it shows more clearly than do newspapers and commercially produced books the relationship of information to its producers. It thereby contributes to the breakdown of dualism.

Since McLuhan published *The Gutenberg Galaxy* in 1962, the question of the relationship between technology and consciousness has been of increasing interest. (For discussions of the effects on human consciousness of the current technological revolution, see, for example, McLuhan, *Gutenberg Galaxy* and *Understanding Media*; Ong, *Orality and Literacy*; and Toffler, *Third Wave*.)

9. I like the definition of *relativism* that Barbara Herrnstein Smith provides in the last chapter of her 1988 book *Contingencies of Value*. In it she explains how relativism has been defined by absolutists as a position either "morally and politically nerveless or logically inconsistent" (Smith 150). The relativism which she advocates "is not a 'position,' not a 'conviction,' and not a set of 'claims' about how certain things— reality, truth, meaning, reason, value, and so forth—really are. It is, rather, a general conceptual style or taste, specifically played out here as (*a*) a conceptualization of the world as continuously changing, irreducibly various, and multiply configurable, (*b*) a corresponding tendency to find cognitively distasteful, unsatisfying, or counterintuitive any conception of the world as fixed and integral and/or as having objectively determinate properties, and (*c*) a corresponding disinclination or inability to use terms such as 'reality,' 'truth,' 'meaning,' 'reason,' or 'value' as glossed by the latter objectivist conceptions" (Smith 151).

CHAPTER 4. LITERATURE IN A GLOBAL SOCIETY

1. Ruthven explains this apparent contradiction as follows: "In the theology of doubt, *jahili* is what fundamentalism is: ignorance combined with the arrogance of religious certainty. Jahilia is where Abraham . . . abandons his wife Hagar in the waterless wilderness. For the devout Muslim, this act of Abraham, the original *hanif* or monotheist, is a commendable instance of his absolute faith in God; for a modern sensibility, nurtured in a universe where ethics have broken free from the religious matrix, Abraham's act seems appallingly callous" (Ruthven 41).

2. Hashemi Rafsanjani made these remarks at a session of the Majlis on February 15: "What one can discern through these events is that there has been planning and organisational work aimed at bringing about a very dangerous move—which is

worse than an officially declared war. Following the blows they received from Iran after the Islamic revolution, as well as following the might of Islam which they saw in Lebanon and Afghanistan and the dynamism and awareness they saw of Muslims all over the world, they arrived at the conclusion, in their analysis, that all this stems from the holiness which covers everything which is sacred in Islam. This keeps the minds of the Muslims clean and gives dynamism and happiness to the world of Islam.

"Materialism and all kinds of political forces failed to break such holiness. So they chose this method of action—choosing a person who seemingly comes from India, apparently is separate from the Western world and who has a misleading name. They begin their work in this fashion. Money had been given to that person, in advance, as royalties. They appointed guards for him, in advance, as they knew what they were going to do. One notes that Zionist publishers are involved and that translations have already been prepared in countries like America and Italy. Such publicity is aimed at preparing the people to buy the book.

"All this speaks of an organised and planned effort. It is not an ordinary work of which one might say that, well, many books have been already written, insults to Islam have been frequent, many others have said bad things against God and everything else and that this is the way in history. Yes, this [is] true. But I believe that there has never been such a well planned act the way it is being done now. This is a confrontation to break the sanctity of Islam and all that is sacred in Islam.

"Therefore, the importance of the issue merits our great leader—who usually does not involve himself in personal issues—involving himself in force to express his anger. It is always incumbent upon us to obey his orders. We always know that he raises issues related to Islam in a timely manner and that he makes a confrontation in due time" (Appignanesi and Maitland 69–70).

3. In late 1990, Rushdie announced that he had met secretly with Islamic scholars and was now embracing Islam; he would support neither an English-language paperback printing of The Satanic Verses nor new translations of the novel. However, according to Time, this announcement prompted no sign of mercy from the present spiritual leader of Iran, Ayatollah Ali Khamenei ("No Mercy for Rushdie" 66).

4. Apparently some fanatics have extended Khomeini's edict to cover those involved in translating The Satanic Verses. The book's Italian and Japanese translators were stabbed in separate incidents in July of 1991; Hitoshi Igarashi, an Islamic scholar and assistant professor of comparative culture at Tsukuba University, died.

5. Sara Suleri says that Rushdie is acutely conscious of the book's status as blasphemy and that he has actually written "a deeply Islamic book" (Suleri 606). She argues that "the text perversely demands to be read as a gesture of wrenching loyalty": "The author well knows that faith is obsolete to his discourse, but must struggle to explain why the betrayal of faith should be so necessary to an unbelieving, postmodern narrative. Such self-questioning makes Rushdie's work far more complex than is

implied by a simple gesture of self-banishment and mockery, illustrating instead its centrality to postcolonial self-fashioning. Blasphemy thus becomes a new and intimate mode of historical introspection; it generates a language of cultural questioning that allows the author to throw up a pair of Muslim hands at the incongruities that impel his discourse, and to elucidate the similarities between the idioms of betrayal and loyalty that history has imposed upon a postcolonial world" (Suleri 607).

6. In the essay Rushdie explains that he opposes *all* orthodoxies: "What does the novel dissent from? Certainly not from people's right to faith, though I have none. It dissents most clearly from imposed orthodoxies *of all types*, from the view that the world is quite clearly This and not That. It dissents from the end of debate. Hindu communalist sectarianism, the kind of Sikh terrorism that blows up planes, the fatuousnesses of Christian creationism are dissented from as well as the narrower definitions of Islam" (Rushdie, "In Good Faith" 53)

7. Michael Walzer, in an essay in *The New Republic*, points out that blasphemy is no longer strictly defined as a crime against God but rather as an "offense against the faithful—in much the same way as pornography is an offense against the innocent and the virtuous" (Walzer 13).

8. Cardinal John J. O'Connor of New York asked Catholics "not to dignify the publication of this work," and Yosef Friedman, an orthodox rabbi, said "the book should be banned. It is offensive to all religions, it's meant to undermine all religious belief." The archbishop of Canterbury, Robert Runcie, urged that England extend its laws of blasphemy, which now cover only Christianity, to other religions (Pipes 163–165).

9. Bilgrami wrote: "The question Edward Said rightly poses and which Agha Shahid Ali is right to quote and ask again—why did Rushdie fall into this Orientalizing misrepresentation of Islam?—therefore, has an answer. In making a 'bad old thing' [pre-Enlightenment religiosity] the target of a post-modern cultural critical stance, *The Satanic Verses* repudiated the historicist restriction of appropriate targets for appropriate stances; it repudiated the restriction as *itself* another Orientalist withholding of the creative possibilities of Islam for its own self-understanding and self-criticism. Why should well-known antecedents to Rushdie within this stance, such as for example the films of Bunilel [*sic*] and Arabal [*sic*] (sickening to devout Christians), be any more justified in their intended power to undermine the seemingly perpetual conserving tendencies of bourgeois European culture than Rushdie's intentions in his own novel, to undermine the constricting and conserving dimensions of the holy for Islamic reform?" (Bilgrami 309).

10. In his *Newsweek* essay Rushdie wrote: "Let me be clear: I am not trying to say that 'The Satanic Verses' is 'only a novel' and thus need not to be taken seriously, even disputed with the utmost passion. I do not believe that novels are trivial matters. The ones I care most about are those which attempt radical reformulations of language, form, and ideas, those that attempt to do what the word *novel* seems to insist upon:

to see the world anew. I am well aware that this can be a hackle-raising, infuriating attempt" (Rushdie, "In Good Faith" 52).

11. *Ethnic separatism* is not synonymous with *multiculturalism*, which represents the acknowledgment of cultural diversity within our population. I use the term *ethnic separatists* for those who wish to preserve the integrity of their particular culture by separating it in some ways from the dominant culture.

CHAPTER 5. THE BACKLASH

1. One of the most vicious of these right-wing attacks is Charles J. Sykes's *ProfScam: Professors and the Demise of Higher Education*, published in 1989. Sykes coined the words "profscam," "profspeak," "profthink," "junkthink," and "bookscam" to characterize the "academic outrages" he presents as typical of professorial behavior. Although the book is unlikely to influence college and university faculty to change their practices, it has contributed to an increasing antiintellectualism in this country, which is making itself felt in the public's support of higher education.

2. During the lengthy debate, senators objected to the inclusion of provisions (2) and (3), which Helms agreed to drop. The Senate then passed the "compromise" bill by voice vote, after voting 65–31 for Senator Wyche Fowler's motion to delete the word "indecent." For more details, see the *Congressional Quarterly Weekly Report* 47 (30 Sept. 1989): 2550, 2569, 2703; also "Tying Down Federal Funds for the Arts," by Marie Tessier, an issue of *Congressional Quarterly's Editorial Research Reports*.

3. The current legal definition of obscenity was established by the 1973 Supreme Court case of *Miller* v. *California*, which classified a work as obscene only if it met all three of the following criteria: "(1) The average person, applying contemporary community standards, would find that the work, taken as a whole, appeals to prurient interest, and (2) the work depicts or describes, in a patently offensive way, sexual conduct specified by the statute, and (3) the work, taken as a whole, lacks serious literary, artistic, political, or scientific value." As Carole Vance points out in her discussion of the NEA controversy, the Miller ruling defined obscenity very narrowly; it did not, for example, prohibit the exhibition of prurient and offensive images if they could be shown to have serious value (Vance 49).

4. Writing in May of 1990, before the reauthorization of NEA and NEH, Vance pointed out that self-censorship in the arts community was already evident and that, because the right wing habitually equated obscenity with sexuality, such censorship would involve not obscenity as defined by the Miller case but rather the expression of sexuality. "The past few months have already made clear that the chief effect of the new [Helms] NEA regulation will be self-censorship by the arts community, both individuals and institutions, encouraged by sporadic episodes of formal censorship

and sensationalized witch-hunts. Last November the *Los Angeles Times* reported that the NEA had held back five literature fellowships because of the sexual or political nature of the projects. In January the *Los Angeles Times* obtained letters written by Sen. Helms to Frohnmayer demanding information about eight arts groups and nine artists over a seven-year period beginning in 1982; the demand seemed motivated by suspicions about the political or sexual biases of the works of those artists and groups. In March, the indefatigable Sen. Helms announced 'compelling' evidence that the NEA had violated the ban on funding obscene art: it had awarded grants to 'three acknowledged lesbian writers.' And most recently, last month, prosecutors in Cincinnati threatened to use the police to remove works that they considered obscene from an exhibition of photographs by Robert Mapplethorpe following unsuccessful conservative attempts to induce the Contemporary Arts Center to censor itself" (Vance 51, 53). On April 7, 1990, Cincinnati's Contemporary Arts Center and the museum's director, Dennis Barrie, were indicted by a grand jury for pandering and use of a minor in pornography. On October 5, after a ten-day jury trial, they were acquitted. (For detailed accounts of the trial see Cembalest, "The Obscenity Trial" and Merkel, "Art on Trial.")

5. Jean Clay, in *From Impressionism to Modern Art*, says that Duchamp, by putting the ready-made object into the New York Exhibition of Independent Artists, introduced a new way of thinking about art: Duchamp showed that "It is the institution that names the object, that decides whether or not it is *art*, that gives it meaning—a meaning, moreover, that can be reduced to the status of a luxury possession, a sign of belonging to a social class, or even a way of declaring the special, elitist condition of its 'creator.' . . . Duchamp's intervention of turning to 'just anything' on sale in a department store shows that everything is 'beautiful' and that if everything is 'beautiful,' nothing is beautiful, that the concept of beauty is not operative, and that the artist's task is first of all to question the institutional enclosure where ideology wants to put him" (Clay 234–235).

6. In an interview with Janet Kardon, Mapplethorpe described his early interest in "pornographic" images: "I went to Pratt, where I did collages. I was also making photographic objects with material from pornographic magazines. At some point, I picked up a camera and started taking erotic pictures—so that I would have the right raw material and it would be more mine, instead of using other people's pictures. That was why I went into photography. It wasn't to take a pure photographic image, it was just to be able to work with more images" (Kardon 23).

7. See Sischy's essay "A Society Artist," in the catalogue to the Whitney show. She writes: Mapplethorpe's "nudes also turn the tables on the work of those artists who have sought to travel outside the image world of the West by portraying what they see as 'the primitive.' . . . Hitler's moviemaker Leni Riefenstahl had that glamour well under her belt, along with a specialized version of these abysmal theories of civiliza-

tion and nature, by the time she ran away on her exotic forays to Africa to photo-graph the people of the Sudan and of East Africa. Piling gilt upon guilt, she brought back her naked-warrior images, thinking—and she was not alone—that they shone with the truth of her subjects' nobility. Instead, her theatrics, her kitschy choices and angles betrayed the fact that she saw these people through those Aryan glasses that seem to have only one end in sight—the creation of an *Ubermensch*. This idea of supermen may arrive in the notion of an army of sophisticated, disciplined blonds purified of 'darkness,' or it may be packaged in a negative of that theme, a vision of darkness as 'pure' nature; or as we see on television and in the movies, it can be some sci-fi construction of unfathomable bionic stuff. However it comes, not far away is the stink of its sickness, of its binary categories of weak and strong, of pure and dirty" (Sischy 79).

8. For Mapplethorpe, it seems, nothing is inappropriate for representation on film. One might note, however, that Mapplethorpe does not record enactments of mur-der (whether on the streets or on the battlefield), battery, rape, or child abuse, all of which are acts of violence regularly depicted in the movies and on television. What Mapplethorpe documents is sexual behavior.

9. Vance points out how censorship turns into self-censorship: "From the censor's viewpoint, self-censorship is an ideologue's dream, since it is cheap, self-policing and doesn't require a large bureaucracy to administer. It is more effective than legal regulation, since fearful individuals, trying to stay out of trouble, anxiously elabo-rate the category of what is likely to be prohibited. Best of all, self-censorship occurs privately, without contentious and unpleasant public struggles" (Vance 53).

10. For a description of NEA's procedures, see Tessier's "Tying Down Federal Funds for the Arts." She explains it as follows: "Once the application is in the hands of the NEA, staff members screen the proposals and prepare recommendations for the endowment's 109 panels of experts, which consider proposals in such diverse fields as modern dance, folk arts, film preservation, opera, stage design and videography. The panelists come from a variety of sources. Some are nominated by state arts agencies, some by current panel members or NEA staff. Some nominate themselves. Ultimately, all panel members are appointed by the NEA chairman. To try to mini-mize cronyism and other conflicts of interest on the panels, the endowment rotates members' terms, so that one-third of the members on any given panel are new each year.

   "After the panels make their funding decisions, the selections are reviewed by the National Council on the Arts, whose 26 members are appointed by the president and confirmed by the Senate. . . . Projects that receive the council's endorsement must then be approved by the chairman of the NEA, who also is appointed by the president and confirmed by the Senate" (Tessier 305, 307).

11. See Roger Kimball's book *Tenured Radicals: How Politics Has Corrupted Our Higher Education.*

12. According to Michael Kelly, writing for *The New Republic*, the orthodoxy may be described as follows: "In its most popular form, 'multiculturalism' holds that the traditional idea of free thought is an illusion propagated by the spoilers of freedom, by the relations of power that obtain in any given society. It holds, more specifically, that the old liberal notion of freedom is only a sentimental mask of a power structure that is definitionally oppressive of those who are not white Western males. And this ideological and methodological principle is not merely a cautionary note to be taken into account when studying the established texts of Western civilization; it is, in the hands of the 'multiculturalists,' the very meaning—the deepest truth about—those texts. . . . The university should therefore be devoted to blowing the whistle on those texts, to replacing them with those that identify and transcend this white male oppression, and indeed go beyond mere study to the actual defeat of the racial and sexual structure of society at large.

"'Multiculturalism' turns out, then, to be neither multi nor cultural. In practice, its objective is a unanimity of thought on campus that, if successful, would effectively end open exchange—exchange that would have to include the alleged representatives of patriarchy—and reduce the nuances of culture to the determinants of race" (Kelly 5–6).

13. See the following for descriptions of the functioning of antiharassment codes on campuses: Lewis, "Friends of Free Speech Now Consider Its Limits"; Wilson, "In Debate on Campus Free Speech, Panelists Consider Wisdom of Colleges' Policies to Fight Harassment"; D'Souza, "Illiberal Education"; Searle, "The Storm over the University"; the December 24, 1990, issue of *Newsweek*; and the February 18, 1991, issue of *The New Republic*.

14. In a May 1991 essay on "P.C.," Catharine Stimpson, a former president of the Modern Language Association, points out that Marxists and progressives had long ago applied the term to party hacks. The term was revived by the right in the late 1980s, when Jeff Shesol, a student at Brown University, made the "politically correct person" the butt of satire in a comic strip (Stimpson A40).

15. It is because nationalism belongs to the dualist model for understanding international relationships that opposition to war appears to indicate lack of patriotism; in the dualist model antiwar sentiment is interpreted as desire to appease the enemy. Since in international competition the government represents the state, opposition to the government's policies, or any form of antiauthoritarianism, can be interpreted as unpatriotic.

The early-1991 rallying cry of the Bush administration, "No more Vietnams," meant not only that the United States would aim for a quick and decisive victory over Iraq but also that it would not allow time for diversity of opinion to develop at home. The "failure" of the United States in the Vietnam conflict was attributed by many politicians and journalists to "disunity" in the American people, lack of patriotism.

1. Darwin also related ethical instincts to the concept of community. In *The Descent of Man* he wrote: "Finally, the social instincts which no doubt were acquired by man, as by the lower animals, for the good of the community, will from the first have given to him some wish to aid his fellows, and some feeling of sympathy. Such impulses will have served him at a very early period as a rude rule of right and wrong. But as man gradually advanced in intellectual power and was enabled to trace the more remote consequences of his actions; as he acquired sufficient knowledge to reject baneful customs and superstitions; as he regarded more and more not only the welfare but the happiness of his fellow-men; as from habit, following on beneficial experience, instruction, and example, his sympathies became more tender and widely diffused, so as to extend to the men of all races, to the imbecile, the maimed, and other useless members of society, and finally to the lower animals,—so would the standard of his morality rise higher and higher" (Darwin, *Descent* 103).

2. Leopold echoes John Stuart Mill, who wrote in *Utilitarianism*: "Actions are right in proportion as they tend to promote happiness; wrong as they tend to produce the reverse of happiness" (Mill 18). Mill was interested in "the good of the whole," which he considered to be human society. Leopold is expanding the notion of the whole to include "the land."

3. In his *Discourse on the Method*, Descartes wrote: "It is also a very remarkable fact that although there are many animals which exhibit more dexterity than we do in some of their actions, we at the same time observe that they do not manifest any dexterity at all in many others. Hence the fact that they do better than we do, does not prove that they are endowed with mind, for in this case they would have more reason than any of us, and would surpass us in all other things. It rather shows that they have no reason at all, and that it is nature which acts in them according to the disposition of their organs, just as a clock, which is only composed of wheels and weights is able to tell the hours and measure the time more correctly than we can do with all our wisdom" (Descartes 117).

4. In his *Discourse* Descartes wrote: "The first of these [precepts] was to accept nothing as true which I did not clearly recognise to be so: that is to say, carefully to avoid precipitation and prejudice in judgments, and to accept in them nothing more than what was presented to my mind so clearly and distinctly that I could have no occasion to doubt it.

    "The second was to divide up each of the difficulties which I examined into as many parts as possible, and as seemed requisite in order that it might be resolved in the best manner possible.

    "The third was to carry on my reflections in due order, commencing with objects that were the most simple and easy to understand, in order to rise little by little, or by degrees, to knowledge of the most complex, assuming an order, even if a fictitious one, among those which do not follow a natural sequence relatively to one another. "The last was in all cases to make enumerations so complete and reviews so general that I should be certain of having omitted nothing" (Descartes 92).

5. Oxford University ecologist Arthur Tansley, who in 1935 coined the word *ecosystem*, argued that *energy* was at the foundation of an ecosystem's structure (See Callicott 106). According to Odum, Tansley considered an ecosystem to be an organized unit. The key concept was "progress towards equilibrium, which is never, perhaps, completely attained, but to which approximation is made whenever the factors at work are constant and stable for a long enough period of time" (quoted in Odum 38).

6. I shall take Ryder as a representative of the position that rights should be extended to nonhuman animals, but of course he is not alone. The Australian philosopher Peter Singer, who had met Ryder at Oxford in the early 1970s, has taken an approach similar to Ryder's in a book called *Animal Liberation*, "about the tyranny of human over nonhuman animals" (Singer i), published initially in 1975 and revised in 1990. Like Ryder, Singer compares "animal liberation" with other liberation movements, whose purpose is to end "prejudice and discrimination based on an arbitrary characteristic like race or sex." And like Ryder, Singer believes that animal liberation represents a widening of the moral circle: "A liberation movement demands an expansion of our moral horizons. Practices that were previously regarded as natural and inevitable come to be seen as the result of an unjustifiable prejudice" (Singer iv). In the first chapter of his book, Singer states that the extension of the principle of equality from one group to another does not necessarily imply equal or identical treatment, only equal consideration. For example, feminists campaigning for equality between men and women do not base their demand for abortion rights on reproductive similarity between the sexes. Singer, who sees sentience as the only justifiable limit to our extension of equality, develops his entire argument, he says, on the principle of the minimization of suffering (Singer 21). A vegetarian himself, Singer asks that each of us stop buying the products of modern animal farms—in effect, boycott—because the animals raised there for meat have not been treated with "real consideration" during their lifetimes. Moreover, in eating meat, even if we are assured that the particular animal we are consuming has lived free of suffering and has died painlessly, we are making another animal a means to our end (Singer 160). Such an act is speciesist.

A plethora of books on our ethical treatment of animals has appeared in the last twenty-five years. See, for example: Ruth Harrison, *Animal Machines* (1964); Monica Hutchings and Mavis Caver, *Man's Dominion: Our Violation of the Animal World* (1970); Stanley and Roslind Godlovitch and John Harris, eds., *Animals, Men, and Morals: An Enquiry into the Maltreatment of Non-humans* (1971); Richard D. Ryder, *Victims of Science: The Use of Animals in Research* (1975); Andrew Linzey, *Animal Rights* (1976); Tom Regan and Peter Singer, eds., *Animal Rights and Human Obligations* (1976); Stephen Clark, *The Moral Status of Animals* (1977); David Paterson and

Richard D. Ryder, eds., *Animals' Rights: A Symposium* (1979); Marion Stamp Dawkins, *Animal Suffering* (1980); Tom Regan, *All That Dwell Therein: Animal Rights and Environmental Ethics* (1982); Harlan B. Miller and William H. Williams, eds., *Ethics and Animals* (1983); Mary Midgley, *Animals and Why They Matter* (1983); Tom Regan, *The Case for Animal Rights* (1983); Peter Singer, ed., *In Defense of Animals* (1986); Steve Sapontzis, *Morals, Reason, and Animals* (1987); Bernard Rollin, *The Unheeded Cry* (1989); Richard D. Ryder, *Animal Revolution: Changing Attitudes towards Speciesism* (1989); James Rachels, *Created from Animals: The Moral Implications of Darwinism* (1990).

7. See Richard D. Ryder, *Speciesism*, a leaflet privately printed at Oxford (1970), *Speciesism: The Ethics of Vivisection*, a leaflet for the Scottish Society for the Prevention of Vivisection, printed in Edinburgh (1974), and *Speciesism: The Ethics of Animal Abuse*, printed for the Royal Society for the Prevention of Cruelty to Animals (1979).

8. In his 1989 book, *Animal Revolution*, Ryder argues that speciesism was written into our language: "Using the word 'animal' in opposition to the word 'human' is clearly an expression of prejudice. So how can this be avoided when describing those sentient creatures who are not of the human species? Does a phrase such as 'animals and human animals' help? It might, but it is rather clumsy. Slightly less cumbersome is the phrase 'nonhuman animal' and its inevitable abbreviation 'nonhuman.' To some this may itself sound speciesist, in that it could be asserting that human is the norm and that nonhuman is inferior. All I can say is that no such inferiority is intended or understood. In the absence of other appropriate words I use 'nonhuman' or 'nonhuman animal' in the hope that their use reminds the reader, as it does me, of the kinship between those of my own species and others" (Ryder, *Animal Revolution* 2).

9. In his 1986 essay, "The Metaphysical Implications of Ecology," Callicott associates himself with Kenneth Goodpaster, who argued in an essay titled "From Egoism to Environmentalism," published in 1979, that mainstream moral philosophy is centered on the individual ego. Goodpaster wrote: "What I am maintaining is *not* that the 'individualistic' model cannot be pressed into service, epicycle after epicycle, to deal with our obligations in matters environmental. Rather my point is that when this is the only model available, its implausibilities will keep us from dealing ethically with environmental obligations and ideals altogether. . . .

"... I am convinced that the mere enlargement of the class of morally considerable beings is an inadequate substitute for a genuine environmental ethic. Once the class of morally considerable beings is enlarged, no hint of a method for assessing or commensurating the newly recognized claims is provided. Nor does it seem likely that it *could* be provided in a nonarbitrary way, given the lack of structure in the model" (Goodpaster 29).

"[I]f an 'environmental ethic' is to be made both genuinely intelligible and morally persuasive, it must abandon a class-membership model of what can count as an 'end-in-itself' or deserve respect. We must, I think, take literally and seriously the possibility that to be worthy of (moral) respect, a unified system need not be composed of cells and body tissue: it might be composed of human and nonhuman animals, plants, and bacteria" (Goodpaster 32–33).

10. Callicott was probably already aware of an essay, published in 1972 in the *Southern California Law Review* and frequently cited, titled "Should Trees Have Standing? Toward Legal Rights for Natural Objects," by Christopher D. Stone, a law professor at the University of Southern California. As Stone explains the occasion, the Sierra Club had in 1971 failed in its suit for an injunction to stop Walt Disney Enterprises from developing Mineral King Valley, a wilderness area in California's Sierra Nevada. According to the opinion handed down by the Ninth Circuit Court of Appeals, the Sierra Club had no "standing" to bring the question to the courts. Knowing that the case was to be reviewed by the Supreme Court, Stone quickly prepared an article for the *Southern California Law Review* to argue that, "If the environment is not to get lost in the shuffle, we would do well . . . to adopt the guardianship approach as an additional safeguard, conceptualizing major natural objects as holders of their own rights, raisable by the court-appointed guardian" (Stone 26). Supreme Court Justice William O. Douglas read Stone's article in draft, having been asked to write the preface for the spring 1972 issue devoted to law and technology in which the article was scheduled to appear. In April 1972 the Supreme Court upheld the Ninth Circuit Court's decision, ruling by a 4-to-3 vote with 2 abstentions that the Sierra Club did not have sufficient "personal stake in the outcome of the controversy" to get into Court. Justice Douglas, joined by Justices Blackmun and Brennan, dissented, and in his minority opinion, in which he cited both Stone's "Should Trees Have Standing?" and Leopold's "Land Ethic," he argued that "environmental issues should be tendered by the inanimate object itself" (Stone 83).

In his essay Stone had introduced what was then viewed as a radically new notion. Instead of asking that the class of persons legally competent to judge pollution of a river, for example, be extended beyond those who could show that it produced an immediate adverse economic impact on them, or that judges look beyond the primary economic or aesthetic impact of pollution of a particular area to consider the threat to the environment, Stone asserted that trees and rivers themselves had "rights." The time had come, he wrote, "when we may have to consider subordinating some human claims to those of the environment *per se*" (Stone 40–43). Acknowledging the difficulty of making a nonanthropocentric argument for the preservation of wilderness, Stone described the pollution of the Earth's atmosphere and oceans as a threat to human survival. But he went on to outline a new nonanthropocentric "myth" for humanity's place in nature: "I do not think it too remote that we may come to regard the Earth, as some have suggested, as one organism, of which Mankind is a functional part—the mind, perhaps: different from the rest of nature, but different as a man's brain is from his lungs" (Stone 52).

11. Upon reading this chapter, my colleague Judy Meyer, a stream ecologist at the University of Georgia Institute of Ecology, pointed out that much ecological work remains somewhat atomistic in its orientation. For example, physiological ecology treats individual organisms; population ecology deals with single species populations; and community ecology has historically concerned itself with studies of competition and predation. She suggests that it is the emergence of ecosystem analysis that is crucial to the development of an ecocentric vision; ecosystem analysis, a branch of ecology, considers biotic and abiotic components of nature together.

12. Gup wrote his essay "Down with the God Squad" primarily to oppose the Bush administration's attempt to amend the Endangered Species Act to allow a politically appointed committee to exempt certain species from protection. The committee, coming to be known in some circles as the "God Squad," would have the authority to determine when human economic interests should override the protection the act granted particular endangered species. Gup is calling the public's attention to the inevitability of conflict between human economic interests and environmental interests when wildlife protection is formulated in terms of either the rights of all species to exist or the value of the preservation of particular species for human benefit. His solution to the problem—to focus on entire ecosystems rather than on single species—is holistic.

13. See Harold J. Morowitz, "Biology as a Cosmological Science," *Main Currents in Modern Thought* 28 (1972). The passage Callicott quotes is the following: "viewed from the point of view of modern [ecology], each living thing is a dissipative structure, that is, it does not endure in and of itself but only as a result of the continual flow of energy in the system. . . . From this point of view, the reality of individuals is problematic because they do not exist per se but only as local perturbations in this universal energy flow. . . . An example might be instructive. Consider a vortex in a stream of flowing water. The vortex is a structure made of an ever-changing group of water molecules. It does not exist as an entity in the classical Western sense; it exists only because of the flow of water through the stream. If the flow ceases the vortex disappears. In the same sense the structures out of which the biological entities are made are transient, unstable entities with constantly changing molecules dependent on a constant flow of energy to maintain form and structure" (Callicott 108).

14. In a critique of "anti-anthropocentric biocentrism," Richard Watson argues that the curbing of human behavior on behalf of the ecosystem represents a positioning of human beings outside of nature and therefore a fundamental anthropocentrism. He says: "To avoid this separation of man from nature, this special treatment of human beings as other than nature, we must stress that man's works (yes, including H-bombs and gas chambers) are as natural as those of bower birds and beavers" (Watson 252). Watson's purpose, however, is to show that anthropocentrism is not only inescapable but reasonable and natural. "There is very good reason for thinking

ecologically, and for encouraging human beings to act in such a way as to preserve a rich and balanced planetary ecology," he concludes; "human survival depends on it" (Watson 256).

Naess replies, in his essay "A Defense of the Deep Ecology Movement," that supporters of the deep ecology movement do talk, in order to make their point, as if human goals should not be privileged over the ecosystem but that their fundamental concern is actually the mediation of needs among humans and nonhumans. He writes: "There is no general norm in ecosophy against our full [human] life in nature, and this implies acceptance of hurting and killing. Ecosophy, as I conceive it, says yes to the fullest self-realization of man" (Naess, "Defense" 270).

15. Naess offers a "platform" for the deep ecology movement:

(1) The flourishing of human and non-human life on Earth has intrinsic value. The value of non-human life forms is independent of the usefulness these may have for narrow human purposes.

(2) Richness and diversity of life forms are values in themselves and contribute to the flourishing of human and non-human life on Earth.

(3) Humans have no right to reduce this richness and diversity except to satisfy vital needs.

(4) Present human interference with the non-human world is excessive, and the situation is rapidly worsening.

(5) The flourishing of human life and cultures is compatible with a substantial decrease of the human population. The flourishing of non-human life requires such a decrease.

(6) Significant change of life conditions for the better requires change in policies. These affect basic economic, technological, and ideological structures.

(7) The ideological change is mainly that of appreciating *life quality* (dwelling in situations of intrinsic value) rather than adhering to a high standard of living. There will be a profound awareness of the difference between big and great.

(8) Those who subscribe to the foregoing points have an obligation directly or indirectly to participate in the attempt to implement the necessary changes. (Naess, *Ecology* 29)

16. *Homeostasis*, as defined by *The Random House Dictionary of the English Language*, is "the tendency of a system, especially the physiological system of higher animals, to maintain internal stability, owing to the coordinated response of its parts to any disruptive situation or stimulus." Homeostatic mechanisms, as Odum explains, are forces and counterforces that operate throughout nature—not only in the individual body to maintain a constant body temperature, despite fluctuations in the environment, but also in the biosphere to keep the relation of carbon dioxide to other gases constant, despite changes in the atmosphere (Odum, *Ecology* 31).

17. Lovelock, who claims to be an agnostic believing in neither a personal God nor an afterlife, is said to have been surprised by the accusations of mysticism and teleology. His colleague Lynn Margulis has expressed disgust with the appropriation of Gaia by New Age mystics (Gardner 255).

18. Botkin lists three concepts of stability important to twentieth-century ecology: "static equilibrium, quasi-steady-state, and classical static stability. Static equilibrium means absolute constancy of abundance of all species over time (like a clock pendulum at rest); quasi-steady-state refers to variations that are persistent but small enough to be ignored (like a shaking clock pendulum); classical static stability has two attributes: constancy unless disturbed, and the ability and tendency to return to the state of constancy following a disturbance (like a pendulum in motion)" (Botkin 42).

19. This is Gould's major argument in *Wonderful Life*. Gould writes: "I believe that the reconstructed Burgess fauna, interpreted by the theme of replaying life's tape, offers powerful support for this different view of life: any replay of the tape would lead evolution down a pathway radically different from the road actually taken. But the consequent differences in outcome do not imply that evolution is senseless, and without meaningful pattern; the divergent route of the replay would be just as interpretable, just as explainable *after* the fact, as the actual road. But the diversity of possible itineraries does demonstrate that eventual results cannot be predicted at the outset. Each step proceeds for cause, but no finale can be specified at the start, and none would ever occur a second time in the same way, because any pathway proceeds through thousands of improbable stages. Alter any early event, ever so slightly and without apparent importance at the time, and evolution cascades into a radically different channel.

"This third alternative represents no more nor less than the essence of history. Its name is contingency—and contingency is a thing unto itself, not the titration of determinism by randomness" (Gould, *Wonderful Life* 51).

20. I use the word *recognition* to indicate that human society was "global" long before we rhetorically acknowledged international interdependence. Imperialism made it so.

CONCLUSION

1. The nickname comes from Lorenz's paper "Predictability: Does the Flap of a Butterfly's Wings in Brazil Set Off a Tornado in Texas?" which he delivered at the annual meeting of the American Association for the Advancement of Science in Washington, DC, on December 29, 1979 (Gleick 322).

2. I believe that Gould's notion of "historical contingency" is a version of the Butterfly Effect. Gould argues in *Wonderful Life* that nature's order "was not guaranteed by basic laws (natural selection, mechanical superiority in anatomical design), or even

by lower-level generalities of ecology or evolutionary theory," but instead was largely "a product of contingency." He writes: "Am I really arguing that nothing about life's history could be predicted, or might follow directly from general laws of nature? Of course not; the question that we face is one of scale, or level of focus. Life exhibits a structure obedient to physical principles. We do not live amidst a chaos of historical circumstance unaffected by anything accessible to the 'scientific method' as traditionally conceived. I suspect that the origin of life on earth was virtually inevitable, given the chemical composition of early oceans and atmospheres, and the physical principles of self-organizing systems. Much about the basic form of multicellular organisms must be constrained by rules of construction and good design. The laws of surfaces and volumes, first recognized by Galileo, require that large organisms evolve different shapes from smaller relatives in order to maintain the same relative surface area. Similarly, bilateral symmetry can be expected in mobile organisms built by cellular division. . . .

"But these phenomena, rich and extensive though they are, lie too far from the details that interest us about life's history. Invariant laws of nature impact the general forms and functions of organisms; they set the channels in which organic design must evolve. But the channels are so broad relative to the details that fascinate us! The physical channels do not specify arthropods, annelids, mollusks, and vertebrates, but, at most, bilaterally symmetrical organisms based on repeated parts. The boundaries of the channels retreat even further into the distance when we ask the essential questions about our own origin: Why did mammals evolve among vertebrates? Why did primates take to the trees? Why did the tiny twig that produced *Homo sapiens* arise and survive in Africa? When we set our focus upon the level of detail that regulates most common questions about the history of life, contingency dominates and the predictability of general form recedes to an irrelevant background" (Gould, *Wonderful Life* 288–290).

Gould shows in his thinking about nature the influence of existentialist philosophy, particularly, I believe, that of Jean Paul Sartre, who developed the notion of contingency in his 1939 novel *La Nausée.*

Works Cited

Albert, Judith Clavir, and Stewart Edward Albert, eds. *The Sixties Papers: Documents of a Rebellious Decade.* New York: Praeger, 1984.

Ali, Agha Shahid. "*The Satanic Verses*: A Secular Muslim's Response." *Yale Journal of Criticism* 4 (1990): 295–300.

Allman, William F. "Nice Guys Finish First." *Science-84* Oct. 1984: 24–32.

Appignanesi, Lisa, and Sara Maitland, eds. *The Rushdie File.* Syracuse: Syracuse UP, 1990.

Aristotle. *The Complete Works of Aristotle.* Ed. Jonathan Barnes. Vols. 1 and 2. Princeton: Princeton UP, 1984. 2 vols.

Arnold, Matthew. *The Complete Prose Works of Matthew Arnold.* Ed. R. H. Super. Vols. 3, 5, and 10. Ann Arbor: U of Michigan P, 1977. 11 vols., 1960–77.

Atlas, James. "The Battle of the Books." *New York Times Magazine* 5 June 1988: 24 +.

Bacon, Francis. *The Works of Francis Bacon.* Ed. James Spedding, Robert Leslie Ellis, and Douglas Denon Heath. 1870. New York: Garrett Press, 1968.

Barthes, Roland. *Image, Music, Text.* Trans. Stephen Heath. New York: Hill and Wang, 1977.

Bennett, A. Hughes, M.D. "Hygiene in the Higher Education of Women." *Popular Science Monthly* 16.28 (Feb. 1880): 519–530.

Bennett, William J. *To Reclaim a Legacy: A Report on the Humanities in Higher Education.* Washington, DC: National Endowment for the Humanities, 1984.

Bilgrami, Akeel. "Rushdie, Islam, and Postcolonial Defensiveness." *Yale Journal of Criticism* 4 (1990): 301–311.

Bloom, Allan. *The Closing of the American Mind: How Higher Education Has Failed Democracy and Impoverished the Souls of Today's Students.* New York: Simon and Schuster, 1987.

Blumenbach, Johann Friedrich. *On the Natural Varieties of Mankind.* Trans. Thomas Bendyshe. New York: Bergman, 1969.

Botkin, Daniel B. *Discordant Harmonies: A New Ecology for the Twenty-first Century.* New York: Oxford UP, 1990.

Bowler, Peter J. *Evolution: The History of an Idea.* Rev. ed. Berkeley: U of California P, 1989.

Brooks, Cleanth, and Robert Penn Warren. *Understanding Poetry.* New York: Harcourt, Brace and World, 1947.

Brooks, W. K. "The Condition of Women from a Zoological Point of View." *Popular Science Monthly* 15.10 (June 1879): 145–155.

Callicott, J. Baird. *In Defense of the Land Ethic: Essays in Environmental Philosophy.* Albany: SUNY P, 1989.

Carnegie, Andrew. *The Gospel of Wealth and Other Timely Essays.* Ed. Edward C. Kirkland. Cambridge, MA: Harvard UP, 1962.

Carson, Clayborne. *In Struggle: SNCC and the Black Awakening of the 1960s.* Cambridge, MA: Harvard UP, 1981.

Cembalest, Robin. "The Obscenity Trial." *ArtNews* 89.10 (Dec. 1990): 136–141.

Civil Rights Act of 1964. Washington, DC: Bureau of National Agencies, 1964.

Clay, Jean. *From Impressionism to Modern Art.* Trans. Arnold Rosin. Rev. and ed. John P. O'Neill and Alexis Gregory. Secaucus, NJ: Chartwell, 1978.

Clouston, T. S., M.D. "Female Education from a Medical Point of View." *Popular Science Monthly* 24.10–11 (Dec. 1883 and Jan. 1884): 214–228; 319–334.

Colaiaco, James A. *Martin Luther King, Jr.: Apostle of Militant Nonviolence.* New York: St. Martin's, 1988.

Craige, Betty Jean. *Reconnection: Dualism to Holism in Literary Study.* Athens: U of Georgia P, 1988.

Danto, Arthur C. "Robert Mapplethorpe." *The Nation* 26 Sept. 1988: 246–250.

Darwin, Charles. *The Descent of Man, and Selection in Relation to Sex.* Vols. 1 and 2. Princeton: Princeton UP, 1981. 2 vols.

———. *On the Origin of Species.* Facsimile of 1st ed. Ed. Ernst Mayr. Cambridge, MA: Harvard UP, 1964.

———. *The Origin of Species.* 6th ed. London: Murray, 1902.

d'Eaubonne, Françoise. *Le Feminisme ou la mort.* Paris: Pierre Horay, 1974.

Decter, Midge. "The Rushiad." *Commentary* 87.6 (June 1989): 18–23.

De Palma, Anthony. "Separate Ethnic Worlds Grow on Campus." *New York Times* 18 May 1991, National, sec. 1: 1 +.

Descartes, René. *The Philosophical Works of Descartes.* Vol. 1. Trans. Elizabeth S. Haldane and G. R. T. Ross. Cambridge: Cambridge UP, 1978.

Dewey, John. "Academic Freedom." *Educational Review* 23 (1902): 1–14.

———. *The Influence of Darwin on Philosophy.* 1910. Bloomington: Indiana UP, 1965.

D'Souza, Dinesh. "Illiberal Education." *Atlantic Monthly* 267.3 (Mar. 1991): 52–79.

Ehrenreich, Barbara, and Deirdre English. *Complaints and Disorders: The Sexual Politics of Sickness.* New York: Feminist Press, 1973.

Ehrlich, Paul, and Peter Raven. "Butterflies and Plants: A Study in Coevolution." *Evolution* 18 (1965): 586–608.

Eliot, Thomas Stearns. *Notes towards the Definition of Culture.* New York: Harcourt, Brace and World, 1949.

———. "Tradition and the Individual Talent." In Eliot, *The Sacred Wood.* 7th ed. London: Methuen, 1950.

Ferré, Frederick. "Obstacles on the Path to Organismic Ethics: Some Second Thoughts." *Environmental Ethics* 11.3 (1989): 231–241.

Fish, Stanley. *Is There a Text in This Class? The Authority of Interpretive Communities.* Cambridge, MA: Harvard UP, 1980.

Fox, Warwick. "Deep Ecology: A New Philosophy of our Time?" *The Ecologist* 14.5–6 (1984): 194–200.

Gleick, James. *Chaos: Making a New Science.* New York: Penguin, 1987.

"Global Village." *Utne Reader* 40 (July/Aug. 1990): 144. Excerpted from *World Development Forum* (15 April, 1990).

Gobineau, Count Arthur de. *Essai sur l'inegalité des races humaines.* Paris: Pierre Belfond, 1967.

———. *The Inequality of Human Races.* Trans. Adrian Collins. New York: Fertig, 1967.

———. *The Moral and Intellectual Diversity of Races.* Trans. H. Hotz. Philadelphia: Lippincott, 1856.

Golley, Frank. "Deep Ecology from the Perspective of Ecological Science." *Environmental Ethics* 9.1 (1987): 45–55.

Goodpaster, K. E. "From Egoism to Environmentalism." *Ethics and Problems of the Twenty-first Century.* Ed. K. E. Goodpaster and K. M. Sayre. Notre Dame, IN: U of Notre Dame P, 1979.

Gould, Stephen Jay. *The Flamingo's Smile: Reflections in Natural History.* New York: Norton, 1985.

———. *The Mismeasure of Man.* New York: Norton, 1981.

———. *Wonderful Life.* New York: Norton, 1989.

Gup, Ted. "Down with the God Squad." *Time* 5 Nov. 1990: 102.

Hagen, Charles. "Robert Mapplethorpe: Whitney Museum of American Art." *Artforum* 27.3 (Nov. 1988): 140.

Haller, John S., Jr. *Outcasts from Evolution: Scientific Attitudes of Racial Inferiority, 1859–1900.* Urbana, IL: U of Illinois P, 1971.

Harrison, John R. *The Reactionaries.* London: Gollancz, 1966.

Henry, William A., III. "Beyond the Melting Pot." *Time* 9 Apr. 1990: 28–31.

Hollinghurst, Alan. "Robert Mapplethorpe." In *Robert Mapplethorpe, 1970–1983.* London: Institute of Contemporary Arts, 1983.

Kardon, Janet. "Robert Mapplethorpe Interview." In *Robert Mapplethorpe: The Perfect Moment.* 2nd ed. Ed. Janet Kardon. Philadelphia: Institute of Contemporary Art, 1989.

Kelly, Michael. "The Derisory Tower." *New Republic* 18 Feb. 1991: 5–6.

Kimball, Roger. *Tenured Radicals: How Politics Has Corrupted Our Higher Education.* New York: Harper and Row, 1990.

King, Martin Luther. *Nobel Lecture by the Reverend Dr. Martin Luther King, Jr.* New York: Harper and Row, 1964.

———. *A Testament of Hope: The Essential Writings of Martin Luther King, Jr.* Ed. James Melvin Washington. New York: Harper and Row, 1986.

———. *Why We Can't Wait.* New York: Harper and Row, 1964.

Kropotkin, Petr. *Mutual Aid: A Factor of Evolution.* Rev. ed. London: Heinemann, 1904.

Lauter, Paul, ed. *The Heath Anthology of American Literature.* New York: Heath, 1990.

Leavis, F. R. *Education and the University.* New ed. London: Chatto and Windus, 1948.

Leopold, Aldo. *A Sand County Almanac.* Intro. Robert Finch. New York: Oxford UP, 1987.

Lewis, Neil A. "Friends of Free Speech Now Consider Its Limits." *New York Times* 29 June, 1990: B9.

Lipman, Samuel. "Backward and Downward with the Arts." *Commentary* 89.5 (May 1990): 23–26.

Lovejoy, Arthur. *The Great Chain of Being: A Study of the History of an Idea.* Cambridge, MA: Harvard UP, 1936.

Lovelock, J. E. *Gaia: A New Look at Life on Earth.* New York: Oxford UP, 1987.

Manegold, C. S. "Robert Mapplethorpe, 1970–1983: On the 1983–1984 Retrospective." *Arts Magazine* 58.6 (Feb. 1984): 96–99.

Mansbridge, Jane J. *Why We Lost the ERA.* Chicago: U of Chicago P, 1986.

Mayr, Ernst. *Animal Species and Evolution.* Cambridge, MA: Harvard UP, 1966.

——. *Evolution and the Diversity of Life.* Cambridge, MA: Harvard UP, 1976.

——. *Toward a New Philosophy of Biology: Observations of an Evolutionist.* Cambridge, MA: Harvard UP, 1988.

McLuhan, Marshall. *The Gutenberg Galaxy: The Making of Typographic Man.* Toronto: U of Toronto P, 1962.

——. *Understanding Media: The Extensions of Man.* 2nd ed. New York: New American Library, 1964.

McMillen, Liz. "Controversial Anthology of American Literature: Ground-Breaking Contribution or a 'Travesty'?" *Chronicle of Higher Education* 16 Jan. 1991: A15, 20–22.

Merchant, Carolyn. *The Death of Nature: Women, Ecology, and the Scientific Revolution.* San Francisco: Harper and Row, 1980.

Merkel, Jayne. "Art on Trial." *Art in America* 78.12 (Dec. 1990): 41–51.

Midgley, Mary. *Animals and Why They Matter.* Athens: U of Georgia P, 1983.

Mill, John Stuart. *Utilitarianism.* Ed. Samuel Gorovitz. Indianapolis: Bobbs-Merrill, 1971.

Montagu, Ashley. *The Idea of Race.* Lincoln: U of Nebraska P, 1965.

——. *Man's Most Dangerous Myth: The Fallacy of Race.* New York: Oxford UP, 1974.

Myers, Christopher. "Arts Backers Are Pleased by Congress's 3-Year Reauthorization of NEA without Restrictions." *Chronicle of Higher Education* 7 Nov. 1990: A19, 23.

Naess, Arne. "A Defense of the Deep Ecology Movement." *Environmental Ethics* 6.3 (1984): 265–270.

——. *Ecology, Community, and Lifestyle: Outline of an Ecosophy.* Trans. David Rothenberg. Cambridge: Cambridge UP, 1989.

Nelson, Cary. *Repression and Recovery: Modern American Poetry and the Politics of Cultural Memory, 1910–1945.* Madison: U of Wisconsin P, 1989.

Nietzsche, Friedrich. *The Gay Science.* Trans. Walter Kaufmann. New York: Random House, 1974.

"No Mercy for Rushdie." *Time* 7 Jan. 1991: 66.

Nott, J. C., M.D., and George R. Gliddon. *Types of Mankind.* Philadelphia: Lippincott, Grambo, 1855.

Odum, Eugene P. *Ecology and Our Endangered Life-Support Systems.* Sunderland, MA: Sinaur Associates, Inc., 1989.

Ong, Walter J. *Orality and Literacy: The Technologizing of the Word.* London: Methuen, 1982.

Patten, Bernard C. "Network Ecology: Indirect Determination of the Life-Environment Relationship in Ecosystems." In *Theoretical Studies of Ecosystems: The Network Perspective.* Ed. M. Higashi and T. P. Burns. Cambridge: Cambridge UP, 1991.

Payne, Buckner H. *The Negro: What Is His Ethnological Status?* Cincinnati: "Published for the Proprietor," 1867.

Phelan, Peggy. "Serrano, Mapplethorpe, the NEA, and You." *Drama Review* 34.1 (spring 1990): 4–15.

Pipes, Daniel. *The Rushdie Affair: The Novel, the Ayatollah, and the West.* New York: Birch Lane Press, 1990.

Pope, Alexander. *An Essay on Man.* Ed. Frank Brady. New York: Macmillan, 1965.

Powers, Richard Gid. *Secrecy and Power: The Life of J. Edgar Hoover.* New York: Free Press, 1987.

Random House Dictionary of the English Language. Coll. ed., 1968. S.v. "holism"; "homeostasis."

Regan, Tom. *The Case for Animal Rights.* Berkeley: U of California P, 1983.

Rushdie, Salman. "In Good Faith." *Newsweek* 12 Feb. 1990: 52–57.

———. *The Satanic Verses.* New York: Viking, 1988.

Ruthven, Malise. *A Satanic Affair: Salman Rushdie and the Rage of Islam.* London: Chatto and Windus, 1990.

Ryder, Richard D.. *Animal Revolution: Changing Attitudes towards Speciesism.* Oxford: Blackwell, 1989.

———. *Victims of Science: The Use of Animals in Research.* London: Davis-Poynter, 1975.

Sancton, Thomas A. "Excellence under the Palm Trees." *Time* 16 May 1988: 74–76.

Searle, John. "The Storm over the University." *New York Review of Books* 6 Dec. 1990: 34–42.

Singer, Peter. *Animal Liberation: A New Ethic for Our Treatment of Animals.* 2nd ed. New York: Random House, 1990.

Sischy, Ingrid. "A Society Artist." In *Robert Mapplethorpe.* Ed. Richard Marshall. Boston: Little, 1988.

Smith, Barbara Herrnstein. *Contingencies of Value: Alternative Perspectives for Critical Theory.* Cambridge, MA: Harvard UP, 1988.

Smuts, J. C. *Holism and Evolution.* New York: Macmillan, 1926.

Stevens, Mark. "Direct Male." *New Republic* 26 Sept. 1988: 27–30.

Stimpson, Catharine R. "New 'Politically Correct' Metaphors Insult History and Our Campuses." *Chronicle of Higher Education* 29 May 1991: A40.

Stone, Christopher D. *Should Trees Have Standing? Toward Legal Rights for Natural Objects*. Los Altos, CA: Kaufmann, 1974.

Strong, Josiah. *Our Country*. New York: Baker and Taylor, 1885.

Suleri, Sara. "Contraband Histories: Salman Rushdie and the Embodiment of Blasphemy." *Yale Review* 78 (1989): 604–624.

Sykes, Charles J. *ProfScam: Professors and the Demise of Higher Education*. Washington, DC: Regnery Gateway, 1989.

"Taking Offense." *Newsweek* 24 Dec. 1990: 48–55.

Tessier, Marie. "Tying Down Federal Funds for the Arts." *Congressional Quarterly's Editorial Research Reports* 1.20 (25 May, 1990): 302–314.

Toffler, Alvin. *The Third Wave*. Toronto: Bantam, 1980.

Vance, Carole. "Misunderstanding Obscenity." *Art in America* 78.5 (May 1990): 49–55.

Vittachi, Anuradha. *Earth Conference One: Sharing a Vision for Our Planet*. Boston: Shambhala, 1989.

Walzer, Michael. "The Sins of Salman." *New Republic* 10 Apr. 1989: 13–15.

Warren, Karen J. "Feminism and Ecology: Making Connections." *Environmental Ethics* 9.1 (1987): 3–20.

——. "The Power and the Promise of Ecological Feminism." *Environmental Ethics* 12.2 (1990): 125–146.

Watson, Richard A. "A Critique of Anti-anthropocentric Biocentrism." *Environmental Ethics* 5.3 (1983): 245–256.

Webster's New Collegiate Dictionary. 1969. S.v. "holism."

Webster's New International Dictionary of the English Language, Unabridged. 3rd ed., 1969. S.v. "west"; "western."

White, Charles. *An Account of the Regular Gradation in Man, and in Different Animals and Vegetables*. London: Dilly, 1799.

White, Lynn, Jr. "The Historical Roots of our Ecological Crisis." In *Western Man and Environmental Ethics: Attitudes toward Nature and Technology*. Ed. Ian G. Barbour. Reading, MA: Addison-Wesley, 1973.

Whorf, Benjamin Lee. *Language, Thought, and Reality: Selected Writings of Benjamin Lee Whorf*. Ed. John B. Carroll. Cambridge, MA: Massachusetts Institute of Technology P, 1956.

Will, George F. "Curdled Politics on Campus." *Newsweek* 6 May 1991: 72.

Wilson, Robin. "In Debate on Campus Free Speech, Panelists Consider Wisdom of Colleges' Policies to Fight Harassment." *Chronicle of Higher Education* 20 Mar. 1991: A35–36.

Woolf, Virginia. *A Room of One's Own*. New York: Harcourt, Brace and World, 1957.

Index